PUT HIM IN,
COACH!

PUT HIM IN, COACH!

A MOTHER'S ALL-STAR MEMOIR

MARTHA PAYNE

iUniverse, Inc.
New York Lincoln Shanghai

Put Him In, Coach!
A Mother's All-Star Memoir

iUniverse books may be ordered through booksellers or by contacting:

iUniverse
2021 Pine Lake Road, Suite 100
Lincoln, NE 68512
www.iuniverse.com
1-800-Authors (1-800-288-4677)

Because of the dynamic nature of the Internet, any Web addresses or links contained in this book may have changed since publication and may no longer be valid.

The views expressed in this work are solely those of the author and do not necessarily reflect the views of the publisher, and the publisher hereby disclaims any responsibility for them.

This book has not been authorized or approved by Little League Baseball. LITTLE LEAGUE is a registered trademark of Little League Baseball, Incorporated.

ISBN: 978-0-595-42782-6 (pbk)
ISBN: 978-0-595-68184-6 (cloth)
ISBN: 978-0-595-87114-8 (ebk)

Printed in the United States of America

For Houston

And for our Little Leaguers, Sam, Matt, and Ian—and yes, Emma, for you, too

There are those who learn after the first few times. They grow out of sports. And there are others who were born with the wisdom to know that nothing lasts. These are the truly tough among us, the ones who can live without illusion, or without even the hope of illusion.... I am a simpler creature, tied to more primitive patterns and cycles. I need to think something lasts forever, and it might as well be that state of being that is a game; it might as well be that, in a green field, in the sun.

—A. Bartlett Giamatti, *The Green Fields of the Mind*

CONTENTS

NOTES & ACKNOWLEDGMENTS XI

BONUS BABY 1

SWING FOR THE FENCES 13

THE PAYOFF PITCH 32

MOMS WHO WOULD BE COACH 44

HEY, NOW, YOU'RE AN ALL-STAR 58

THE BRUSHBACK 71

TEAM MOM TO BE 84

THE SHOW 102

A LITTLE EXTRA BP 119

DUCKS ON THE POND 133

THE BOYS OF SUMMER 146

MOPPING UP 167

Notes & Acknowledgments

Half of all proceeds from sales of this book will be donated to RBIs, Reviving Baseball in the Inner Cities, a program sponsored by Major League Baseball and instituted in major cities across the United States. Initial proceeds will support equipment purchase, field maintenance, and the hiring of umpires for Atlanta's Junior Braves Baseball League, an RBIs outreach program implemented by the Atlanta Boys and Girls Club and designed to teach the value of teamwork, encourage academic achievement, and foster self-esteem among minority and other youth by providing them the opportunity to play organized baseball.

Due to the limitations of memory, I took occasional liberties in the structuring of scenes in this book, especially with regard to the unfolding of play-by-play action in specific games. At times, I combined or streamlined events and dialogue, yet the events recounted here are true in the sense that they did happen at some point during my son's youth baseball career. With a few exceptions, names have been changed to protect the privacy of friends and colleagues.

I'd like to extend special thanks to the three coaches whose names I've used directly. You know who you are. Your names remain because for you, there can be no substitutes. You've meant the world to my sons. Many thanks also to my friends and fellow mothers without whose support this book would be neither lucid nor particularly funny. All the times you drove extra carpools or entertained my children (many never repaid), you were freeing me up to write, and rewrite. A few others—Diana, Hollis, Janice, Missy, and Sharon—deserve a special nod. Thanks for your brilliant ideas, editing expertise, and encouraging words. Finally, thanks to all the many members of my extended family—especially to my mother and my late father, for giving me life and a love of words, and to my husband and children, for giving me a story to tell.

—Martha Payne

Bonus Baby

Not altogether by coincidence, I turned up pregnant a couple of weeks after my oldest son completed play in his first Little League all-star tournament. Already a mother of three, I was thirty-eight, old to be expecting again, at least in broad, universal terms, though only slightly past my prime in this day of fifty-year-old celebrities conceiving miracle babies. My friends, long finished with 2 AM feedings and diapers, felt both relief and a twinge of regret over this happy news. Though the idea of another infant exhausted them, most of them teared up to think of that baby powder smell or the touch of a downy cheek. They marveled at the bravery and generosity of spirit my husband and I demonstrated in choosing to bring yet another life into the world. They comforted themselves by blaming our slightly outrageous behavior on my Roman Catholic upbringing—"Oh, you're from such a large family," they exclaimed. "Naturally you'd want lots of children of your own!"

This was true, I agreed, trying to *feel* brave and generous, smiling through the hormonal hangover that plagued me, wondering, secretly, why anyone would *volunteer* to endure three months of feeling nauseated at the smell of coffee brewing or the mere sight of raw poultry. And why was it again that I thought I needed to reengage in such domestic challenges as chopping Vienna sausages into bite-sized pieces or wiping mashed banana off of countertops? Years before, my husband and I had seemingly achieved parenting nirvana—two nascent bundles of male virility for him, a sweet little princess for me—and soon they would all three be enrolled in a full school day.

What was I thinking?

In retrospect, a protracted series of hormonal moments may have been responsible, yet there I was, the specter of forty hovering at my doorstep, and pregnant, committed once again to the joys of breast pumps and infant drool and soon to embark on hundreds of additional nights of half-sleep. Worst of all, I would before long become one of those preschool moms that everyone mistakes for Junior's grandmother.

Why did I do it?

I couldn't get enough of Little League baseball.

◆   ◆   ◆

Ah, you're still reading, which can only mean you fall into one of three categories: you're a non-parent with a sick interest in neurotic parental behaviors; you are a Survivor, the adult child and possibly primary caregiver of such a neurotic parent;

or most likely, you yourself are a parent somehow familiar with a condition the journalist Bill Geist, a victim of the malady himself, once called *Little League Syndrome*, a syndrome found commonly in parents of boys who play Little League baseball but now recognized in several other mutations as well, among them *Pop Warner Football Fixation, Gymnastics Flip Fever,* and *Youth Soccer Syphilis* (so dubbed because its effects on the adult human brain are far-reaching and in most cases, irreversible). If you are the parent of a more cerebral or creative child, you may suffer from one of a family of related yet slightly higher-brow parenting addictions lovingly known as *Drama-Mama Disorder,* or even *Youth Symphony Shock Disease.*

The names are different, the symptoms the same: brash and inappropriate behavior at games, auditions or concerts; constant, nagging phone or e-mail communications with busy coaches or bandmasters; micromanagement of the lives of children who would be better served spending their afternoons biking through the neighborhood or playing in a ditch; and finally, bouts of melancholy at the conclusion of a given athletic season or performance schedule, characterized most often by insomnia resulting from the endless mental replay of a child's performance, *if only …*

But I'd wager most of you can breathe easy because, honestly, would even the least stable among you consider having another child to fulfill your own wretched dreams? I ask not for your pity, only your attention, maybe a suspension of your disbelief while I recount one woman's story of total immersion in all things Little League. Who knows—maybe some of you will be shocked yet entertained by the myriad ways an otherwise decent mother could allow herself to be drawn into the tangled web of such a condition, but I suspect some among you may find solace in these pages, maybe even join me in what I like to call Mommy Rehab, because that's where I am and will remain, and God knows, it's a protracted and endless battle.

As with most psychiatric disorders, my problems started early. Though I don't exactly blame my parents, or my place in the birth order, I feel that in the spirit of self-analysis and do-tell-all psychology popular today, I must begin there, at the beginning, when I myself was only a high-strung, Type A competitor-waiting-to-happen. I grew up in the 1960s and '70s, an era when only the *best* athletes on a team got trophies, only the *smartest* kids received academic awards. Being the youngest child in a family of six, I clutched at any opportunity to divert my parents' attention from matters involving my older siblings, and I discovered early that nothing garnered their love and attention like an honor or an award. In my mother's case, *Happiness Was* … a report card glowing with As.

Perhaps more important to my case, however, is the fact that I grew up in a household drenched in testosterone. My one sister, sixteen years older (and a talented swimmer, by the way), vamoosed before I was old enough to cut a paper doll, much less dress a Barbie. Through no fault of her own, she left me in the care of four older brothers. My mother, a *lady* to the core, tried her best, but all female role modeling aside, I was a born tomboy for whom edging out the competition, any competition in any form, brought great personal satisfaction. By the time I was eight, I preferred a game of HORSE on our driveway basketball hoop to playing house or attending the ballet classes Mom insisted on. I never missed a minute of the *Wide World of Sports* on Sundays, and I spectated loyally at my brothers' sporting events. One of them was the star of his high school basketball team—during each of his games, my parents and I made an unnecessary fuss whenever he swooshed a foul shot or performed some complicated dribbling maneuver while paying not a spec of attention to the poor kids warming the bench. It was all very damaging, I'm sure.

But as is generally the case with young impressionable girls, my most questionable tendencies with regard to sports, and to baseball in particular, can be traced back to my relationship with my father. He had season tickets to Georgia Tech football games, and while my mother shopped or went Antiquing, I would sit happily above the fifty-yard line, flanked by Dad and a couple of brothers. I cheered and analyzed strategy and quickly learned the meaning of a P.A.T. and a clipping penalty. A graduate of Tech, my father taught me the words to the Ramblin' Wreck fight song, even the beloved curse of the archrival. In those days, nothing thrilled me more than to shout, "To hell with Georgia!" with no risk of having my mouth washed out with soap. A few years later, I enjoyed the early days of *Monday Night Football*—a sporting event to watch on a school night, what a novelty! This was such a special occasion, I was allowed to flop on the living room floor at Dad's feet and do my math homework in front of the television.

A few months before I turned six, the Milwaukee Braves moved to Atlanta, and Dad took to listening to games on his AM radio. A businessman whose exercise regimen consisted of several hours of weekend yard work, he liked to turn on the ignition in his Oldsmobile, roll down the windows, and crank up the Braves' play-by-play while he trimmed hedges and weed whacked. I'd shoot baskets or play nearby, within safe earshot of the easy hum of Ernie Johnson's commentary.

Finding his sons engrossed by then in the vagaries of teen life, Dad began taking me out to the ballpark. Sporting caps adorned with a funky (and decidedly non-P.C.) tomahawk, we latched on to Braves' players like Rico Carty and Felipe Alou. Together, we admired the Cat, Felix Millan, who could turn a double play with the grace of a feline. Our hearts quickened to see Hank Aaron's strong, fluid swing launch pitch after pitch into the seats. Yes, we enjoyed the competition, the *game*, but there was more. Baseball was ours alone. My father sitting strong and tall beside me, I came to love the game's slow, almost drawling pace, the dramatic unfurling of each inning, the long, lingering season. Like Dad, I was a fiercely loyal but easily disappointed fan. There was great comfort, then, in the fact that in baseball, if things didn't go your team's way, another game would be quick in coming, possibly just minutes after the final out, or at the very least, the next day.

So maybe this—a passion for the game—later instigated my fanatical behavior. It's reassuring to think so. And maybe it wasn't thoroughly unwholesome that when my firstborn son, Sam, four years old, picked up his plastic bat and whiffle ball and asked me to pitch to him in the backyard, I fell in love. To that point, Sam and I had struggled for a mutual interest, for some bond stronger than the instinctive ties between mother and son. Being the family of a surgeon-in-training and living in a strange city, we were often lonely. We needed each other, but mothering small children did not come easy for me. I was by nature a loner, a reader and a thinker, more teacher than nurturer or playmate. Sam, like most boys, was a bundle of restless, random energy, a talker who craved distraction and attention, hands-on and lots of it. But on that first day (and many after), I found I was content—no, more—I was *happy* to pitch to Sam.

As whiffle ball after whiffle ball sailed high into the blue Georgia sky, a sense of deep satisfaction would quell Sam's restless nature. Now and then, he would drop his bat, blonde hair a rumpled mess, gaze after his hit with cherubic green eyes, and jump with glee as I chased into the farthest hedge to dig out the ball. "Mommy, Mommy! Watch out for snakes!" he might yell, smiling, before standing in again, bat cocked behind his soft little shoulder, ready for my next pitch.

Thus did Sam and I find a place to play, together.

A couple of years and several split and dimpled bats later, I signed him up for tee-ball. He quickly demonstrated a knack for the game, and before long, my healthier maternal emotions were sublimated—how did this happen?—as I began my descent into mania. Watching an older Sam slam line drives and make diving catches in the field fulfilled me in a way other aspects of parenting did not. Like any first-time mother (or like most, perhaps? *a few?*), I thrived on hearing my fellow parents marvel at my son's natural grace and talent. I dreamed blissfully each night, my baseball-consumed brain replaying his triumphs on the diamond like an ESPN highlight tape. Soon, our second son, Matt, began slugging away himself. Eventually, because I found I couldn't bear the thought of missing even a single one of my boys' games, I organized family meals and outings around their Little League schedule. Who needs planetariums or zoos when you've got fields of grass to play on? And nutrition be damned—my toddler daughter could eat hot dogs and popcorn for every meal if it meant I could cheer on my boys.

During his nine-year-old season, Sam posted a set of career stats, and coaches began to take note of his skills. He pitched well and batted over .600, which means he had a hit two out of every three times he came to bat. Top professionals are paid seven-digit sums to average above *.300*, but in Little League, only those who reach base nearly every time they step up to the plate stand apart. And Sam did it! You can imagine my euphoria. At the end of this season, he was rewarded with an election to the All-Star Tournament Team. Having heard of his acceptance to Yale University couldn't have given me more of a high, a high which only stoked my obsessive tendencies. *I'd* always known Sam was all-star material. *(I was his mother!)* Thus, I never doubted he would excel in tournament play.

He didn't. Far from it. No, Sam came up short of expectations in almost every category. Given the position of starting center fielder because of his speed and agility, he misjudged fly ball after fly ball. Known for his intelligent approach to the game, he flailed through a series of mental errors. Famous for reaching base often and being a good contact hitter, he struck out about half the time.

Desperate for the comfort and isolation of our whiffle ball afternoons, I soon developed a tic, a little twitch of the cheek with each swing-and-a-miss. Not long after, my idle fingers discovered the joys of neurotic pill rolling. And nail biting was a given. Before the district all-star tournament was over, the anguish of watching Sam fail and the embarrassment attendant on my body's small betrayals drove me away from my post as cheerleader. Rather than witness Sam's dreary, droop-shouldered shuffle back to the dugout after a strikeout or an error, I left the bleachers where other mothers gloried in their sons' prowess and sweated out his games on a mosquito-infested hillside above right field.

Ever the lioness, I tried to blame his coaches, blood-thirsty men who kept dropping him in the batting order—how would he ever gain experience and boost his self-esteem if he batted last? Sam needed a coach who believed in him, not one who would shower him with expletives after he popped out on a bunt attempt. He was only nine years old, for heaven's sakes. He simply needed time—and understanding!—to develop into the next Babe Ruth.

Late in that all-star season, my nightly highlight tape morphed into a nightmare of first-time mother stress. I would replay images of Sam fumbling a fly ball or whiffing at a fast pitch and blame myself for the downcast look on his tender face as we drove home. Then the *what ifs* began—what if his self-confidence couldn't recover from this failure? What if he were (God forbid) to quit baseball?

And so, for reasons of posterity and self-preservation, I began to consider the option of an insurance policy. Our first three kids appeared to be thriving in spite of my limited parenting skills, and at thirty-seven, all my reproductive parts seemed in good working order. My husband, however, was a hard sell. As an MD fully aware of the risks involved in birthing healthy babies (particularly for the more mature mother), Houston felt plenty fulfilled by our brood. Yet, like most men, he is somewhat short-sighted and pleasure-oriented…. Let's just say with a little coaxing, he began to think more of the means to my desired end than the final outcome.

We thus embarked on what may seem a risky venture. Say this new babe inherited none of his father's remarkable hand-eye coordination, or only a meager ration of his grandfather's quickness and dexterity? Could it be that his genetic coding would resemble more that of his grandmother (who once walloped herself in the forehead during a leisurely game of croquet) than those of his athletic siblings?

What if junior turned out to be another girl?

This seemed hardly a problem. During her brief stint on earth, our daughter, Emma, had proven to be as coordinated as her brothers, perhaps even more so. Though gymnastics was her sport of choice, a second daughter might well take up softball. Yet even in the early weeks of my pregnancy, my mommy-meter indicated that we'd managed to conceive our third boy—another shot at the big leagues. *Boys run in my family!* And darn if I wasn't right. Our eight-and-a-half-pound son, James Ian, burst into the world just hours after his due date. He pushed and hurried his way out so that I nearly had to give birth without benefit of anesthesia.

"Good!" I reasoned breathlessly through clenched teeth. "He'll be quick. And aggressive!"

"This one's got a set of lungs!" the nurse noted as Ian's howls pierced the antiseptic silence of the delivery room.

I smiled, noting the strength of his screeches even as I surrendered to the twilight sleep brought on by my epidural in the final hour. I dreamed of our new babe stepping up to bat in Tom Thumb—sized baseball cleats only to rip a home run off of the ten-year-old giant who pitched to him.

"A ten. And a nine point three!" A vaguely familiar voice tore me out of my reverie. Dopey with exhaustion, I struggled to comprehend.

"His APGAR—a *ten*, and a nine point three!" Houston repeated, tapping his index finger repeatedly on a computer printout where presumably these crucial numbers appeared, numbers that the pediatrician had assigned Ian at birth, numbers that supposedly measured alertness, strength of reflexes, general well-being.

As the nurse laid Ian's warm, soft, somewhat gooey body over the slack ruin of my belly, Houston squeezed my forearm. "Those are really high scores!"

The night's labors must have been wearing on him, too. As a rule, he responds to life's triumphs with much the same scientific, matter-of-fact approach he does its tribulations. He certainly had never before shown excitement in public over something as pedestrian as one of his children's APGAR scores.

Draping my hands over my latest born, I pulled my lips into a wilted smile before drifting into a contented slumber. Another child had arrived, whole and hearty, and I realized with a jolt of shock that I didn't particularly care what Ian's APGAR scores were, that unlikely as it seemed, what I'd wanted all along wasn't a baseball player but a child. I suppose tangled within the dendrites of my competitively wired nervous system, I possessed a hint of a maternal instinct after all.

Still, Ian's scores were *really* high! They could not be ignored!

Besides, unlike my husband, I am a pedestrian, non-medical type, a sucker for such a significant numerical ranking, the first my son would achieve in a life that would no doubt *teem* with them. Most assuredly, such strong numbers would one day translate into dexterity! Energy on the athletic field! A high slugging percentage!

And energetic Ian certainly was—an early riser whose thirty-minute naps provided more annoyance than relief in our frantic days. He walked late, however, posing a significant worry. Sam and Matt had walked before they hit ten months, Emma at a year exactly, but Ian showed no interest in getting up and going anywhere until he was nearly thirteen months old. My cheek twitched.

"Oh, he'll probably just be a genius," quipped my mallet-happy mother, who merely tolerates my fascination with sports. "Might be musical. Or artistic! We could use an artist in the family."

Now there's an interesting prospect, Mom. Sort of like me as a ballerina. Sadly, drawing *stick* people can be a trial for me. Never do I feel more inept as a parent as when one of my children has a project that requires sketching anything more complicated than a cube. But sure, an artist. I could get used to that. I'd spend afternoons hanging Ian's latest masterpieces in our gallery née garage rather than keeping up with the number of hits he'd had or bases he'd stolen.

Ian did finally walk, of course (long before he wielded a crayon, by the way), but he did something else first—something I surely dreamed when he was in utero and by maternal powers instilled in him. He pitched. At nine months. OK, OK, victims of the syndrome tend to exaggerate. Ian threw a tennis ball, but he achieved such extension in his elbow and chucked the thing with such force, you could only call it a pitch.

And his first word?

Ball.

He was a dream come true! And we had six years, his brothers and sister, Houston and I—six full years!—to mold him into a competitive baseball player. How could we miss? By the time Ian reached legal league age for tee-ball, I would have guided Sam through seven years of Little League. Then double that to account for Matt and his youth baseball career.... I'd be nothing less than brimming over with experience.

I didn't know the half of it.

SWING FOR THE FENCES

In many ways, not least among them his having been born last, Ian was gifted with a certain edge over his older brothers. Ask any seasoned youth baseball coach to list the factors he weighs most heavily when creating his list of top prospects before draft day, and among them, no doubt, will be the following, not necessarily in this order:

- Older brothers?
- Hand-eye coordination
- Mental focus
- Is he youngest brother in family?
- Speed and agility
- Coachability (and other intangibles)
- Paternal Personality Index (*Ideal*: coordinated enough to throw BP; not overly zealous)
- Maternal Personality Index (*Ideal:* athletic and organized, yet slightly clueless. Stay-at-home moms preferable. Hot? See *Team Mom*.)

- *Older brothers in Little League?*

You can see how Ian might stand out. But Sam, poor Sam, had little to fall back on save his God-given talents, and I spent many a sleepless night after that first (sub-par) all-star season of his, worrying that I'd waited until he was *six* to consider signing him up to play tee-ball. Inconceivable! There I was, a naive first-time mother raised in an era when even your burliest jocks tended to put off organized sports until maybe age ten—how was I to know of the rich opportunities out there for the pre-school athlete? Besides, it seemed I woke one day just after finally figuring out how to load his Little Tikes pop-up pitching machine (ages two to four), and Sam had grown so tall, he had to crouch down like a pint-sized version of Jeff Bagwell in order to swing.

It didn't help that our little family had been on the move. During Sam's preschool years, we lived in three different cities with varying levels of enthusiasm for kiddie sports. He dabbled in soccer here, wasted a precious spring season learning lacrosse there. Most of Sam's future all-star teammates, meanwhile, had been firmly based in Atlanta, where they enjoyed a couple of preliminary seasons of church-league baseball before entering Little League.

Sadly, we moved into the city only a few months before Sam turned six and became eligible to play *real* Little League-sanctioned tee-ball at Frankie Allen Park, home of Buckhead Baseball, Inc. We lived only a few miles from Frankie Allen, and I was raised in Buckhead, a geographical district considered a suburb in the days before Atlanta's metropolitan area encompassed about a hundred counties across North Georgia. Nowadays, Buckhead, or *Buckhead Village*, as it is known by the trendy twenty-somethings who frequent its establishments, has become a hub of Atlanta nightlife.

Yet as history goes in the American South, Buckhead has a colorful past. During the 1840s, legend has it, near a forested crossroads just northwest of what would later become Terminus, then Marthasville, and finally Atlanta, a tavern owner named Henry Irby one day hunted down and killed a buck—a strapping, prize-winning sort of buck. Proud and plucky, Irby (one of whose descendants played ball with Sam 150 years later) hung the buck's bloody head on his hitching post. Before long, every farmer in the county was meeting *at the buck's head* for social hour.

Despite these inauspicious origins, Buckhead developed into the closest thing Atlanta has to a Beverly Hills, with affluent neighborhoods growing up around a quaint retail center. Throughout the first half of the twentieth century, Tara-like homes on rambling lots and grand churches sprouted up along a four or five mile stretch of Peachtree Street. When I was a preteen in the early 1970s, my friends and I were allowed our first independent journeys into Buckhead to shop at the Sears Roebuck or grab a bite of lunch at a fountain drug store. In my earlier years, I toddled behind mother and brothers to places like Buckhead Hardware and the Buckhead Men's Store, a crusty old establishment where graying men in dark suits knelt down with measuring tape to deck out their youthful customers for Sunday services. I also skipped alongside when Dad stopped in to watch my brothers play Little League at a place then called Bagley Park, located about a half mile east of the former site of Henry Irby's tavern.

In the 1980s and '90s, Buckhead reinvented itself. Commercial development ran amuck and much of the area's charm gave way to an inevitable urbanization as Atlanta grew rapidly into an international city. Today, sleek high-rise condominiums populated by young professionals or retirees (mostly from points north) have replaced all but one of Peachtree's mansions. A new Starbuck's sprouts up every other month, and a swanky restaurant featuring two-inch-thick steaks stands where my Sears once did. Traffic moves along Peachtree so thick and fast that no mother could in good faith allow her child the freedom of bicycle travel. Besides, cheesy nightclubs line the strip that once housed establishments like the Buckhead Men's Store, and every few months, the proprietors of Buckhead's nightlife somehow manage to extend closing time. I think it's currently four AM, which provides lots of extra time for shootings and prostitution and all sorts of other seedy activities to occur. Old Henry Irby, as fond of drawing a pint as he was, might be a touch disturbed.

When time came for Sam's first Opening Day, I awoke itchy with anticipation and had everyone ready to head for Frankie Allen a good hour before game time. Our then family of five buckled securely in our minivan, we pulled onto park grounds, carefully skirting the huddle of homeless women that like to kick back at the picnic tables near the entrance, then rolled past one, then another, clay-colored infield, each freshly raked and smoothed, with newly etched foul lines glistening. Ancient pine trees and scattered hardwoods provided pockets of shade over the bleachers and outfields, whose dew-sprinkled grass, spring green and fragrant with a recent mowing, glittered in the chilly March sun. Adjacent to home plate on the Majors' field rose a concession stand decorated with red and blue balloons, and beyond right field was a set of authentic batting cages where twelve-year-old sluggers crushed baseballs against chain-link fencing.

Tucked between the Majors field and its batting cages, the tee-ball diamond stood gallantly in a far corner of the park, as far as possible, I noticed, from the entrance and its vagrants (what a relief for the concerned tee-ball mom). Below the out-field, a hillside fell sharply away towards the rear of the park where Buckhead's yuppies liked to walk and exercise their dogs. This orientation, I would soon learn, made for primo excite-ment when a superstar tee-baller managed to hit a ball over the fence. It could roll for yards and yards, only to be retrieved hap-pily by some young stock broker's Labrador. But as time would tell, there aren't all that many true, over-the-fence home runs in tee-ball. You might see four or five in an entire season, a statistic my Sam couldn't quite swallow. As we motored slowly past the field hunting for a parking spot, he lamented the fact that he hadn't been able to hit a homer himself during pre-season prac-tices.

"Mark's hit three already!" Sam whined, his blue belt buck-led on the last notch to cinch in his baseball pants, size youth extra-small yet roomy, considering Sam's lack of girth. His cap adjuster likewise was crossed over at the back, in vain as it turned out

"One of them landed way over there," he said, bill of cap slipping over his eyes.

His head held at a precarious backwards tilt, Sam pointed to an azalea bush to our right. Wild and unkempt, its blossoms were just before bursting into fuchsia.

"Well, Mark's a bigger kid than you, honey," I answered.

"Size doesn't have that much to do with it," Houston quipped.

Thanks, dear. Read any child psychology lately?

"I bet you'll hit one out before the season's over!" he added and I had no choice but to punch my husband's thigh.

"Now he'll be overswinging all the time!" I whispered.

"I won't, either, Mommy," Sam said, all ears.

"Well, you need to focus on being an all-around player anyway," I said. "There's more to baseball than hitting."

"Quit touching me, Matt!" Sam yelled, shoving his little brother against Emma's car seat where Emma herself, four months old, nestled in deep sleep.

"Ow!" Matt cried, eyes filling with artificially rendered tears. "Mom! His *fingernails* are touching me!"

"Shhhh! You'll wake the baby," I said, reaching back to pat Matt's knee.

"Dad says nice and easy swings get the biggest hits," Sam the Daddy-pleaser, continued. "Everybody knows that."

Houston grinned in satisfaction as he wedged the van into a makeshift parking space, and we unloaded, all a-twitter with excitement.

Game one pitted Sam's Braves against the Tee-Rockies. Sam came to bat in the first inning after the soon-to-be-famous Mark had rounded the bases on a towering fly ball that did not, in fact, go over the fence but might as well have—it bounced against said fence and lay there ignored by the Rockies' outfielders until their parent-umpire finally trotted out to fetch it. Sam then cracked a solid hit up the middle, sending the ball bouncing through the shortstop's legs and on past two outfielders, one of whom was facing the wrong direction, watching one of those friendly retrievers lope after a Frisbee on the road below.

"Pick up the *ball!*" came the gruff command from the Rockies' dugout, and ten little faces turned towards their livid coach as if to say, "Now there's an idea!" (This coach would later be banned from tee-ball for his *intensity* on the field.) Meanwhile, Sam raced around the bases, bareheaded, of course, his cap having flown off somewhere along the first-base line. It looked as if he might follow Mark into the dugout with an inside-the-park homer of his own until the Rockies' first baseman, clearly talented and clearly determined to stop this circus act, turned on his jets and bolted from first to the center-field fence. He scooped up the ball and made a rocket throw to the third baseman, who in an act of self-preservation, allowed the ball to ricochet off his body as Sam dove back to third. In awe, I watched the first baseman run back to his post and noticed for the first time a ponytail bouncing through the gap in his—uh, her—cap. Yes, the play which reminded the Rockies they were playing a baseball game rather than enjoying a day in the park was turned by a girl, one who robbed Sam of his first full trip around the bases. Not so good for his tender ego.

"Nice hit, Sam!" I yelled, clapping heatedly in an effort to deflect any potential feelings of ineptitude. After all, a triple in his first at-bat—nothing to sneeze at! I turned to my fellow mothers, feeling sure they were impressed with my firstborn. Instead, they were red faced with muffled laughter, hands clasped over mouths. When I turned back to the field, I saw Peter, our next batter, running headlong at Sam who was trying to dodge him to make it safely home. Peter had hit the ball well enough to score Sam but then, sadly, had chosen to run up the third-base line.

"Go the other way!" hollered Jim, our normally mild-mannered coach. "Towards first, Petey! That way!"

Jim, who stood in the coach's box a mere five feet away from Peter, gestured in the direction of first base, but to no avail. A speedy little devil, Peter was already halfway to third, nearly eye to eye with Sam, and here came Little Miss Rockies over from first again. Ball in glove, she tagged both boys out for a double play.

And I'd been warned that watching tee-ball was like watching paint dry. Blasphemy! In a single inning, I'd gone from nervous excitement to exhilaration to emotional languishing—it was better than the *real* Braves.

◆   ◆   ◆

The Buckhead Tee-Braves developed into a huggable little team that failed to win a single game that first season, despite Mark's power hitting. Dubious though the distinction may have been, Sam did become one of the stars of his team. Although the other parents never said this in so many words, Houston and I could sense it. We could sense it in the curious way Gus, the most competitive dad among them, set his teeth as he whacked Sam on the shoulder as a means of congratulating him after a big hit. We could see it in the watery eyes of the mother whose son could hardly hold the glove above his head in the effort to catch a pop fly. Glancing our way on the bleachers, she'd whisper, "Thank goodness for Sam," who'd just leaned in to catch a fly ball inches behind her son's unprotected head. At that point, it seemed to make little difference that Sam had

missed those seasons of preschool ball. He could scoop up way-
ward balls deflected off of less attentive players, snag line drives
(rare though these are in tee-ball), and throw with the grace of a
dancer.

Methinks the lady doth boast too much, but reader, forgive
me. The flesh is weak and now and then the urge to indulge my
parental bias too strong. Sam's tee-ball glory was so delicious.
And, ah, so fleeting. Now that I have eighteen years of parenting behind me, I know how hard being *good* at something really
is for kids today. Successful high school athletes drag into
weight rooms at 6:00 AM (before classes) in order to keep up
with the competition. But first-time parents don't know this,
and even if they do, it doesn't matter—nothing tops the thrill of
witnessing a child first revealing a natural talent, be it a pen-
chant for sports or an ear for music or a gift for comforting others. You know it when you see it. It comes unbidden, and
nothing is more beautiful to a parent than its purity and effort-
lessness.

Truth be told, Sam's illustrious tee-ball career spoiled us.
During the late games of the Buckhead Tee-Braves' second season, Houston and I began to take for granted the doubles and
triples and RBIs, even the circus catches, that Sam seemed born
to execute. We grew bored, antsy for the day our son would
graduate to what's known as the Rookie League, not quite real
baseball but close enough for the eight-year-old slugger. In
rookie play, the batter stands in at home plate as he would in
traditional baseball and waits for an umpire to feed a ball into a
pitching machine, thus insuring more consistency of pitches for
the developing hitter.

About three minutes after Sam received his second tee-ball
trophy, I began to dream, day and night, of Sam's future domi-

nation over this machine. These dreams sustained me through yet another dreary, cabin fever-infested winter completely devoid of baseball. Then, early one Saturday in mid-February, I roused before any child seized the chance to infiltrate our bedroom. Perhaps it was the scent of crisper, drier air, a slight evaporation of winter's mucky mold, but something moved me towards the window, where the rays of a sun beaming more strongly than the day before were peeling back the thick skin of gray that had gripped our city since early November. In the backyard, crocus and daffodil buds were beginning to push open in happy response. Everywhere, rodents and birds and other suburban wildlife were shaking off the drowsiness of winter to begin a new season of foraging and reproducing.

A modicum of warmth, the promise of new life ... baseball on the horizon. My children too caught a hint of renewal in the air and rustled early. Down the hall, Emma chattered with the bunny who was her cribmate while Matt scrambled in his costume trunk to find Superman's missing cape. Moments later, Sam, bat in hand, raced through our bedroom door clad in his fresh-issue Little League uniform.

"What time do we go, Dad?" he called, unaware that his father still lay drenched in sleep, slightly less anxious than the rest of us to emerge from winter's long nap.

"Practice doesn't start 'til ten, sweetie," I whispered. Emma began demanding rescue from her crib, but I ignored her, glad for a moment to bond with my firstborn.

"*Aaww*, that's like ..." Sam glanced at the clock, pouncing on Houston. "... more than three hours away! Dad, can we go early? You could pitch to me!"

"*Never* wake me this early!" Houston growled in mock anger, rolling over to tickle Sam.

"No, Dad! Stop!" Sam cried.

"Of course. Early it is," Houston added, tickling all the harder.

Ahhhh, the pre-season—there is surely no happier time for the Little League family. Such promise wafts in with the warming air … and so much to do! There is the new bat to be purchased, slightly longer and heavier than last year's to account for the added power a year's growth will guarantee, and the new cleats to be sized to accommodate increased speed on the bases. Uniforms fairly glisten and coaches are all sunshine, smiling and promising not only a championship by season's end, but equitable playing time and candy rewards for stellar performance and open channels of communication with parents. The highlight of February for me personally is finally getting my hands on the game schedule, then recording in my calendar every last opportunity I will have to cheer on my brave slugger. In short, nothing stands in the way of a star being born.

But something went wrong. Very, *very* wrong.

At practice that day, the machine wound up, pitched, and Sam swung and missed. A lot. He *struck out*. Again and again, in fact. And not only on that ominous day, but deep into his Rookie season. The umpire on the mound would hold a ball aloft, and Sam, arms quivering, soft small knuckles aligned on the bat, would blink, his cap tipping ever so slightly to indicate his eagerness, his determination. This time, he would hit it. This time, he would earn the right to show off his speed on the bases, perhaps even to *slide*. How he longed to slide—to smudge and stain those sleek white pants! As the ump dropped the ball into the machine's hurling mechanism, Sam would coil back his bat, unleash his beautiful left-handed swing, and catch air. Again and again.

Maybe it was the machine itself, I reasoned. A metal contraption on four spindly legs, it is a decidedly cold, menacing thing, inhuman and featureless save for a dark hole resembling a mouth, a monster's mouth, that spits out balls at what must seem a breakneck speed to a child accustomed to having his parent pitch to him. Maybe Sam needed to witness the human exertion of a pitcher's windup to better predict the trajectory of that little white ball. Or maybe, just maybe, it was divine retribution, the baseball gods giving us our due for the sin of pride.

The psychological strain brought on by Sam's failure in the face of the monster machine turned out to be simply a primer for the gut-wrenching lows that are an integral part of parenting a Little Leaguer. Slumps, or extended periods of poor performance, are all part of the ball game, unless you happen to have one of those kids with such built-in self-confidence that he or she doesn't think twice about having struck out in his last two at-bats when he steps up to the plate the next time around. He simply believes this time he will get that hit. *Who me? I'm not in a slump—I'm due!*

I spent much of Sam's Rookie season greening up with envy of the mothers of such boys, watching brazenly their interactions with the young Ty Cobbs they seemed to be raising. After all, I reasoned time and again, I can be taught! If emulating these supermoms would help me infuse my sons with confidence, then I'd study their parenting skills until the stadium lights went dim. No doubt I should have long ago purchased a self-help book (or a hundred) on this topic, but what Little League mom has the time? There are practices to be watched, strategies to formulate!

And besides, how could Sam control what seemed written in his genes? He was jockish, yes, but also a sensitive and analytical child. How could he help but apply these traits to his own play? And apply them he did. He would strike out once, come up to bat later wearing a look of edgy hope, swing once, twice, thrice, and strike out, again. *He's not using his legs,* his coaches might advise, *not throwing his hands, not following through … He's thinking too hard!*

That was it! At age eight, he'd already overengaged his cerebrum, lost his boyish playfulness. And while he deliberated and analyzed, his previously less-talented and blissfully less self-aware cronies sprayed machine-pitched balls all over the place, infield and out. Heck, when Sam's younger brother played in the Rookie League, he saw not a monster in that machine but an ally. Matt struck out once, exactly *once,* in his fourteen-game season.

During this endless Rookie charade, I would bite my lip, toss back my hair, and watch Sam's shoulders slump after each strikeout until they finally held in a slouch for the duration of each game. Houston and I forced smiles and thanked our fellow parents for their continuing encouragement. Gus, the shoulder-slapping dad from Braves' tee-ball, was again one of our fellow parents. In fact, Sam generally batted behind Gus Junior who by midseason had developed one of the hottest bats on the team. I suspected Sam's coach, Jim, the same nurturing, mild-mannered man who'd guided Sam to his tee-ball eminence, was trying to take the pressure off of Sam by letting him bat after a boy whose hits would more often than not clear the bases.

One day, Gus Junior came to bat with the bases loaded and, sure enough, hit a triple to the fence. When Sam swung and missed for the third out, stranding Gus Junior at third, Big Gus caught me broadside with that meaty paw and gave me a wink.

"Don't worry. He'll get that magic touch back soon!"

I winced.

"Some of 'em have trouble making the transition from the tee to a live ball," he continued, doling out another thud between the shoulder blades.

'Preciate the tip, Gus, but it's all on account of that cursed machine!

Against all reason, Houston and I grew quite popular that season, as if the more glaring Sam's weakness became, the more attractive we were as a family. Perhaps the baseball gods needed something more than game day humiliation, something harsher, more along the lines of a burnt effigy. Thus, we were invited to cook out with people we hardly knew. What could we do but accept and stuff our miserable faces as Sam dragged along his albatross of a bat, then swung and missed right in his friends' own backyards?

As the Rookie season drew to a close, Sam began to get the knack of the monster's trickery. But the machine would not give up so easily. Although he began to pick up a few hits, most of Sam's hardest-hit balls shot right back at the evil ball-spitter (was this accidental?). He'd slam a line drive in the direction of center field, and the ball would careen off the metal leg of the machine. Guess what that meant? Dead ball. It touches any part of the machine itself, and you lose. No credit given—replay!

In spite of this, Coach Jim refused to give up on Sam. When asked by the Rookie commissioner to name two players to an all-star team, he chose his own son (a solid, all-around player) and Sam. After all, he may have had a weak bat, but Sam was still *the man* in the field.

Houston and I missed that early June all-star game—as I remember it, against my will. Had I known before season's end that an all-star game or team even existed, I never would have planned to go along on his annual fishing trip for tarpon. *I don't even fish!* But it was too late to change our plans. Sam's grandparents went to his game in our stead.

"How'd Sam do?" I spat into the hotel phone, my ear sweaty with Florida humidity.

"He played just fine. Fine," answered my perpetually optimistic father-in-law.

"Did he get to bat?"

"Uh, just once or twice, they had him a ways down in the batting order." (*Dead last*, Sam told me later—not that I was surprised.)

"And?" I just knew he'd broken through, showed 'em his stuff after all.

"I can't quite remember. Wasn't on base much."

He struck out, of course. *Twice.*

Yet I entered that off-season with hope in my heart. Sam's coach knew Sam still had the spark. He'd been named an all-star, after all! But that was before I figured out the truth. Being dubbed an all-star is one thing. Being elected to the *All-Star Travel Tournament Team* is quite another thing altogether.

◆   ◆   ◆

One afternoon the following fall, a familiar rap sounded on our front door.

"Sam home?" asked the impish boy from down the street.

"Sure, come on in, Jack," I answered. Our customary exchange, Jack and I, only rarely embellished upon to something more intimate like, "How's your mom?"

But I paused that afternoon before returning to the freezer where I'd been shuffling through Ziploc bags of raw chicken and ground chuck. Jack wore a ball cap I didn't recognize, not his usual—the green one highlighted with a distasteful boar's head in full snort with fangs bared, team mascot of the Rookie Warthogs. Last season, Jack's (and his dad's) Warthogs played for all the marbles in the Rookie championship game. Jack had ever since been fond of wearing his Warthogs cap when he visited our house. No doubt, he enjoyed reminding Sam it was largely his ineffective performance in the face of the monster machine that had kept his Rookie team ten victories shy of that tournament game.

But today's cap was different—no endangered species with teeth or whiskers here. This cap was classy, even elegant, you might say. Upon its royal blue crown, embroidered white stars encircled a Gothic *B* in muted red.

"Is that Pete's old cap?" I asked, though I knew a kid like Jack would never deign to wear one of his older brother's hand-me-down caps. A perceptive boy, Jack took note of my perhaps inappropriate curiosity, and before answering tipped his head back so that the late afternoon sun glinted on the stars, revealing the wisp of a silver border carefully etched around each one. By age nine, in spite of his scrawny build, Jack had starred on at least four baseball teams. He *knew* the significance of the cap. I wondered if he hadn't switched leagues on us—had he been drafted to play on one of those teams out in the suburbs where the *real* competitors go? It even crossed my devious maternal mind that Sam might have a better chance at Buckhead stardom with Jack *gone.*

"Naa. All-Stars," Jack offered, grinning. Bored now, he took a single graceful leap across the foyer and bounded up the stairs.

I paused a moment, hand on the doorjamb, late October sun warming my thighs, trying to make sense of this, until Emma toddled near, threatening to tumble down our brick steps. Still bewildered, I scooped her up and returned to my freezer.

The All-Stars? Sam had no special cap from his play in the all-star game. I'd asked him about that, in fact, when we returned from chasing tarpon in the Gulf of Mexico the previous June.

"No, we just wore our regular jersey and cap," he'd replied meekly. He'd been embarrassed, no doubt, to show his face in his native garb, painful reminder of his fatal flaw.

So what did it signify, this celebrated *B* on Jack's cap? Not Braves. I knew all too well the cursive lines of that *B. Bears?* More of a football or hockey monogram. *Bucks?* Could be. Ah, that was it, of course. BuckHEAD, a cap fashioned to honor once again the taxidermic triumph of good ol' Henry Irby. A *B* encircled with stars. The all-stars would simply be the Buckhead All-Stars. No mascot needed for such a prestigious team.

But why didn't Sam have a cap?

"Jack's on the *Travel Team*, Mom," he informed me at the dinner table that night. "It's totally different," he added with that roll of the eyes I came to know so well as he edged into his teen years.

"Travel team? Where do they go?"

"How should I know?" he answered, shoving back from the table. "I'm full," he said though he had just sat down to his chicken and rice. He stood and cleared his place while I resisted the urge to force more body building calories into his small frame. How would he ever surpass Hank Aaron's home run record on four bites of poultry?

Research later revealed that after the Rookie all-star *game*, the better half of the boys involved had been promoted to the *real* all-stars, the *travel* or *tournament* team, the terrific twelve, boys who'd looked the monstrous pitching machine square in the eye and slammed out hits and runs all season long. When they hung up their team caps in early June, these chosen ones had doffed the *B*-studded lid and begun a whole new season. Under the leadership of a handful of the most voracious regular-season coaches, they'd practiced for two weeks in June and played in a district tournament. Thus, they *traveled* to another baseball park for summer tournament games, and then *traveled* again during September and October to yet another park to play a round of weekly fall games. Their baseball off-season lasted only eight weeks tops, meaning they (and their parents) got at least a dozen extra games, not to mention the expert training they received from those top-notch coaches.

It wasn't fair! How would Sam ever catch up?

Perhaps it was boredom with my domestic lifestyle, nine years of nuking hot dogs and watching Barney the purple dinosaur dance around on his oversized T-Rex feet that pushed me ever nearer obsession. Or perhaps I was guilty of a sin common in parents—snatching at another chance to gain personal recognition by cashing in on my child's talents. After all, I'm a product of the 1980s—an intelligent woman with a post-graduate degree! I could have been a lawyer, or a marine biologist or, or, Diane Sawyer! But I'd chosen to *stay at home*. If my children didn't grow up to be perfect, wouldn't that imply that all my parenting blood, sweat and tears had been shed in vain?

No matter the reason, the image of Jack's blue, *B*-studded cap perched askew on his scruffy head of hair that October afternoon became my serpent in the tree. From thenceforth, in the autumn of my thirty-eighth year, I drifted slightly out of the realm of emotional normality. Call it hormonal hysteria if you like, but I would not rest until Sam was chosen to play on a Buckhead Tournament Team.

THE PAYOFF PITCH

I launched my campaign the following Christmas, figuring that would give me a solid month to work with Sam before tryouts, plus another six weeks until Opening Day of his AA season. I began by filling his stocking with useful paraphernalia: batting gloves, a baseball signed by Chipper Jones, a free pass for an hour-long hitting session at an indoor batting cage. And under the tree? For Sam, of course, there was a new bat, one whose length-to-weight ratio I'd carefully researched to jive with his height and the diameter of his biceps.

"Wanna try it out?" I asked him well before his focus could wander to the Hot Wheels loop-de-loop and the arsenal of Nerf guns his impulsive father had insisted on.

"Uh, sure, Mom. Thanks," he said, smiling feebly and pulling the gloves over his pale, thin fingers.

Sam liked his bat. Like most nine-year-old boys, he liked baseball. A lot. But he liked being a kid, too, enjoyed playing Nintendo and riding his bike and shooting baskets with his buddies in the school gym where it happened to be *warm*. Lest we forget, Christmas comes in December, and even in the South, December is cold. That's why no one plays much baseball then. Although Sam shivered through a few swings of his new bat that Christmas morning, I have to admit, for the most part, he resisted my off-season efforts to hone his hitting skills. You might even say he resented them.

None of which phased me. Neither wind nor ice nor threat of player burnout could dampen my enthusiasm for the development of his baseball potential. In fact, I came up with a brilliant idea. Around mid-January, I noticed the children suffering from winter's malaise. Bored with their Christmas loot, they whined daily to be allowed more television time, more videos, more handheld electronic devices. Solution?—a field trip! On a damp, chilly Tuesday afternoon, I pried Emma, three years old, away from her post as parlor maid to a dolly tea party and strapped her into her car seat next to Matt, always caught in the middle.

"Where're we going?" he complained, squirming against Sam, whose left thigh had been strategically angled deep into his span of vinyl. "I'm missing the *Power Rangers* special!"

"Yeah, Mom. It's too cold," Sam said, legs resolutely spread-eagled.

"To find tennis balls!" I answered, perhaps a bit heavy on enthusiasm. "We're gonna have a little BP!"

Sam cut his eyes at me, something like a scowl across his gentle features. Was it his batting average he contemplated? Or his mother's sanity?

Emma banged her tiny feet on the oversized empty paint tub I'd tucked beneath her seat.

"What's this bucket thingy, Mommy? I don't like it!"

Matt tugged at the tub, catching the blunt edge beneath Emma's calf and eliciting an appropriate wail.

"Leave it alone," I ordered, buckling my seat belt. "It's to collect the balls in."

In the rearview mirror, I saw Sam nudge Matt with an elbow and shrug in my direction. Thus he quieted the others in that way that only the oldest child can, and only when the silencing results in a feeling of some instability, that they'd better shut up lest Mom really go off the deep end.

Once we unpiled at the local high school tennis courts, all was well. It was fun, searching under moldy leaves and overturning piles of trash to find as many abandoned tennis balls as we could. We found brand-new ones, soggy ones, even a few that had suffered such erosion they were left feltless.

"Should we take this one, Mom?" Sam asked, holding up a sphere of little more than nubby rubber.

"Sure! Bet you'll hit that one the farthest of all!" I ventured. And thunk, it landed in the tub.

My plan was this: each afternoon after school until Opening Day, I would pitch Sam at least one full tub of tennis balls. I'd done some reading in a Little League coaching book at the local bookstore (furtively, of course, not wanting to raise suspicions). Repetition is the key to good hitting, I'd learned. A coach does the young player the most good by encouraging as many daily swings of the bat as possible. These can be swings off the tee, swings in a batting cage, and yes, swings at tennis balls. Furthermore, with enough repetition, the player will achieve *muscle memory*.

Hmmm. That could mean only one thing. Sam's muscles could memorize what to do when the ball spun across the plate and get a hit every at-bat. Thus would I make a hitter, a regular Pete Rose, out of my firstborn.

Tryout Day arrived, a cold but bright Sunday in early February. Though Sam bit his nails during the ride to the park, I felt confident. By then, approximately 347 tennis balls lay just where I wanted them, frozen deep in the patch of ivy behind our neighbor's formal garden, a good fifty or sixty yards from the makeshift home plate I'd fashioned in our somewhat shabbier backyard. I found a parking spot, wished Sam luck as he ran off, glove and bat hugged to his slender torso, and gathered together my coat and sunglasses and the NASCAR sleeping bag I'd tossed in at the last minute, then trotted to the frigid AA bleachers. Once there, I settled in to watch Sam perform. On my right was a mother more knowledgeable than I, one whose eldest son had already advanced to the mighty Major Leagues. As her secondborn, a *B*-studded all-star cap on his head, ripped a line drive over the third baseman's glove, she frowned, rubbing her chapped hands together, then lamented, "I hate when he has such a good tryout."

Not wanting to appear unschooled, I groped for the appropriate response but managed only a sigh that fogged her sunglasses.

"You know," she went on, politely polishing her shades. "It's better if a coach drafts them lower than they should go, unless your son's good enough to carry the whole team."

I smiled, nodding. Apparently, I had a lot to learn.

We turned back to the field where Sam stood in to hit, his nose and cheeks red with cold. He glared bravely at the monster machine and managed to lay down a few hard foul balls, yet struck out nevertheless. My heart sank, yet in one sense, how clever of him!

"Just like we planned!" I said.

My wise neighbor eyed me askance.

"You know," I said. "His dad and I suggested he hold back a little."

As if to emphasize the wisdom behind this pronouncement, bold-faced lie though it was, I took a jaunty step towards the dugout, leaving Mrs. Been There, Done That, gaping after me, wondering for sure how good this Sam-person really was.

What she'd hinted at was a devious technique employed by a number of Little League parents. If Johnny has a weak tryout, all but the most informed coaches will rank him as a less skilled player than he actually is. He may then be drafted in a late round and end up with a powerhouse team—a coach might take a number-one pick, followed by numbers two and possibly even three, finally followed by Johnny, a number one simply masquerading as a number four. Some parents will go so far as to keep their budding Albert Pujols home on Tryout Day—*Can't make it today, a bit under the weather!* such parents (one of whom inevitably comes to tryouts anyway, just to see how things go) may lament, always within earshot of the entire regiment of coaches. Thus, only the coach who knows the ill child (the one the parent *hopes* will draft him) recognizes Johnny as the ace player he truly is. The others will rank him low and the preferred coach gets a future Pujols for a song.

Although Sam's weak hitting during his tryout had twisted my belly into a hopeless kink of frustration, it did serve a certain purpose. Rather than being gobbled up by a ruthless (albeit championship-hungry) coach, he was drafted by Coach Jim, the same fair-minded man who'd coached him in tee-ball and the Rookie League. Plus, Coach Jim, heretofore dubbed the Fair-Minded, waited a bit to claim Sam, waited until after he'd drafted two tournament team all-stars, which meant he'd managed to acquire *three* all-stars for his AA Cobras, seeing as how

Sam *was* an all-star at heart, even if only his mother knew it at the time.

All we lacked was a fresh tub of tennis balls.

◆   ◆   ◆

By Opening Day, my efforts seemed to have paid off. Sam had become so adept at clobbering those tennis balls, he could now lock in on the baseball as it left the pitcher's hand and make sound contact most of the time. His hand-eye was back. And those lean little biceps had achieved muscle memory! It mattered little that the baseball went not quite so far as those hundreds of tennis balls. The baseballs were going nonetheless, and Sam, well, Sam believed. In his first game, he hit a double, which his speed stretched to a triple. I smiled and wiped away a tear.

"Nice hit," said Annie McMillan, alias Mrs. Been There, Done That, whose son Walter had been one of those traveling all-stars Coach Jim drafted first.

"Thanks," I said. "He's been working on his swing."

The weather on that Opening Day was not so kind. It *sucked*, to borrow a phrase from the now teenaged Sam. As is frequently the case, the winds of March had blown Atlanta onto the cusp of a late-season Arctic Express, the inevitable result of that pesky jet stream that enjoys dipping down to about the Florida state line in early spring, trailing behind it frigid winds and a bone-chilling drizzle.

You can imagine, then, how unpopular Opening Day can be. In fact, all but the most intensely loyal moms and dads hate it. It's not just the interminable tee-ball parade or the long-winded speeches by commissioners and city councilmen that precede the command to *play ball!* Attending Opening Day usually results in significant physical discomfort. Yet parental attendance is mandatory. How cruel and unjust it would be to register a child for Little League, force him to go to practice throughout the sodden month of February, and then send him off in cap and glove and long underwear to play uncheered.

Rather than dread Opening Day, however, I sleep little the week before, embroiled as I am in frantic expectancy. The sense of well-being I felt that day as I nestled under my sleeping bag on a splintery bleacher seat to watch Sam seemed almost gluttonous. How quickly we mothers forget! A few short months before, I'd excused myself regularly from the convivial atmosphere of those seats and scavenged for a patch of dirt near the outfield fence where I cowered to watch Sam strike out to end nearly every game. Now I sat proudly, perfectly centered in the row, feeling smug and sure of my son's multifaceted gift. While I'd spent the winter months homeschooling him on the finer points of hitting, his coaches had discovered a hidden bonus—he had a decent arm. On that frigid Opening Day, Sam was the team's starting pitcher.

We had the last AA game of the day—first pitch, five-thirty. The damp air seemed to have surrendered every skinny calorie of warmth to a low-slung gray sky. Though the thermometer read forty-seven degrees, the wind chill, as I recall, registered twenty-nine. Our AA Cobras emitted nervous groans when it was their turn to take the field. For the first time in their young lives, the weaker players considered themselves lucky to be asked to sit out an inning or two in the dugout, where the team mom had sneaked in hot chocolate and extra parkas to ward off pneumonia. The unfortunate Cobras who were forced to play in the field as the sun sank on this day when snow flurries, parents began to whisper, had just been forecast, looked shell-shocked. Shivering, teeth chattering, they moved in slow-motion, hardly able to throw the ball across the infield.

Yet Sam's face showed determination, even desire, rather than anxiety. Was that self-esteem I saw rising in his psyche? Or was he simply better dressed than his teammates? He did have a certain edge, a little secret only a mother could know. At age nine, one of Sam's favorite pastimes was watching the Weather Channel. My budding meteorologist had been tracking this particular cold front for three days. No surprise, then, that he wore under jersey and pants not one but *two* layers of long underwear, plus a turtleneck and two pairs of socks. Those who watched closely would see him now and then reach into the back pocket of his pants with his pitching hand. There I had placed a pocket hand warmer, the type intended for skiers and ice climbers, while inside each cleat was tucked a toe warmer. Whereas I'd forgotten the day before to pack his lunch for school, I could never be accused of being unprepared for a baseball game.

My entire brood, in fact, looked like we'd just stepped off the set of a photo shoot for L.L. Bean's winter catalog. Matt wore a parka and a pair of ski pants designed for subfreezing temperatures atop his own layers of long underwear and ski socks and mittens. Emma sported multistriped leggings in the brightest colors with a sweater to match, all tucked under a hot pink ski bib and jacket (and we don't even ski!). Pulled tightly over her blond head so that only her nose and a pair of green eyes peeked through, was a fleece-lined wool cap complete with ear muffs in hot pink splashed with purple flowers. Although she had considerable trouble climbing the bleachers, Emma was *warm*. She and Matt quickly became the envy of Sam's shivering teammates, most of whose faces seemed frozen in a shudder of discomfort as they huddled up before the first pitch.

"This is ridiculous," croaked Marie, the Cobras' number one sports skeptic, the same mom who at the preseason parents' meeting had asked whether the boys would be provided with protective eyewear when they batted.

"I mean, what coach—and father!—would have our sons play under these conditions?" she demanded between sips of coffee from her handy thermos.

I winced, seated as I was next to the coach's wife, she herself prone to be concerned in these situations but also a loyal fan and wife. As she cleared her throat to speak, I rushed to her rescue, providing what seemed a logical excuse.

"The coaches don't have any control over this. The games have to be cancelled by the AA commissioner," I said.

"Walter's Rookie team finished out a game last year in a driving rainstorm," added Mrs. Been There, Done That. "We won and then went to the championship."

Marie shrugged, anything but convinced.

"The guys really don't have a choice but to play," I ventured. "Unless we want to forfeit the game."

Marie glared, her eyes like bullets, and parted her lips to speak, her mind no doubt conjuring all the many barbs she could employ to highlight my shortcomings as a mother (need I mention Marie and I had found ourselves in such a confrontational pose before?). But she restrained herself, drew a curtain over those bullet-eyes as if to dismiss my opinion as hardly worthy of consideration.

"Heaven *forbid* we forfeit a game!" she thundered instead, turning back to the field where just then Sam zinged in a pitch that the opposing batter managed to foul off for a strike.

"Ow!" yelled the batter as the cold aluminum bat vibrated mercilessly in his tender hands, then dropped to the tundra-like dirt.

Where were this boy's batting gloves?

"Foul ball!" the umpire called, rubbing the child's limp, bare hands before handing him his bat. The boy wiped away a tear, arms and knees trembling, yet stood in to take the third strike.

"That's it. I'm taking Joshua home," exclaimed Marie, peeling away the cocoon of blankets across her lap. She marched to the end of the dugout and flung both arms over her head to wave down Coach Fair-Minded. One look at her and Jim called time and brought Josh in from right field, without so much as a word with Marie. Josh packed up his extra clothes and left, head hanging yet with a clip in his gait as he hurried to catch up with his mother.

"Play ball!" came the cry from the ump as another unlucky Cobra emerged from the womb of the dugout, bracing himself against the outfield winds.

"Mommy, my nose is cold. Can we go home?" Emma begged, tugging on my Gore-Tex mitten as best she could manage in her mummy-like apparel.

"Not quite yet, sweetie," I said and patted the purple pom-pom atop her hat. As I pulled off one mitten to reach for a Kleenex with which to wipe her drippy nose and watery eyes, I felt a twinge of nausea and something resembling respect for

Marie's resolve. Briefly, I even worried about my children's health. I glanced at Matt—though his cheeks flamed with windburn, he seemed alright, nimble enough in his skiwear to run around with friends and generate body heat. Yet Emma's woeful pink frown induced a pang of Mommy guilt—was this a reasonable way to treat a preschooler? Even more to the point, would pitching in such cold weather endanger Sam's arm?

I could feel my fellow Cobra moms squirming in a similar manner, all of us struggling with that most powerful of maternal discomforts, the one that inevitably raises its ugly head when another parent does something that we know we might do ourselves were we stronger willed.

"Mo-mmmy," Emma whined, tugging relentlessly. "My toes are froze! *And* I need to go pee-pee!"

Oh, Lord, not now, I thought. Stripping her down to use the toilet would take the rest of the inning. I folded over my own tightly bound middle to reassure her, just as a shout from the opposing team's bleachers cracked through the icy air.

"We'll go in a minute, Emma," I snorted, jerking my shameful head towards the field.

It was a fly ball! For the bad guys! I caught a glimpse of Sam as he kicked the rubber and slumped his shoulders. But it was a lazy, high fly ball that carried slowly towards ... *yes! Right field! The spot Josh had just vacated!* I jumped from my seat, catching Emma's jaw with my elbow and knocking her sideways on the bleacher. Josh's replacement, Ben, perhaps more alert than usual from the shock of the cold that had yet to permeate his bones, looked skyward and zeroed in on the ball. He moved a step to his left, stretched his glove above his head, supported it with his free hand, and made the catch for out number three.

An outfield catch in AA ball is a rare event, and yet little Ben of the Cobras had done it—and during an Arctic Express!

The bleachers erupted in utter mayhem. We moms were positively giddy, jumping and hooting and hugging each other like long-lost friends. How we pitied Marie. *And poor Josh!* He could have made the catch of his life if only his mother had shown a little backbone. Sam leapt and frolicked on the mound, relieved that what might be the only well-hit ball of the game had actually been fielded by one of his teammates. His catcher came out to embrace him as the first baseman and center fielder and Coach Fair-Minded did the same for Ben.

I scooped up Emma, wiping her tears with my glove the best I could.

"Look at Sam, Mommy!" she whimpered. "He's getting squished!"

"No, he's fine, honey. They're just happy!"

"Yay, Sam!" she yelled, then, "Ooops, Mommy. I think I pee-peed."

"We'll clean you up at home," I whispered, continuing to cheer, determined that nothing should ruin this moment of Little League glory.

Moms Who Would Be Coach

Behind the leadership of Coach Fair-Minded and his past and potential all-stars, the AA Cobras finished strong. Sam pitched and hit well throughout the regular season, and as a result, I demonstrated the sunniest of maternal dispositions. I was, in fact, a paradigm of emotional equilibrium, not only because of my son's performance, but because early in that AA season, I had made a crucial discovery.

"Look at this!" called Laura, mother of the Cobras' first baseman, as I approached the bleachers before game three. "It's my latest lineup!" she continued, thrusting a funnel of printer paper under my nose.

Trembling, I unfurled the funnel and studied what looked to be a computer-generated analysis of the Cobras' varied talents. Stapled cozily behind was a spreadsheet displaying suggested positions where each boy might excel in the field.

I smiled, my heart metabolizing a heretofore unmatched level of joy.

"I think Jim may actually use it!" Laura gushed, and with that we launched into the first of hundreds of strategic sessions about who should bat leadoff and cleanup, and which boys Coach Jim should at all costs avoid playing at shortstop. In the months (and years) that followed, Laura and I were sometimes accused of taking Little League too seriously. *Poppycock.* Maybe we were a smidge more competitive than your average mom, but we had in mind the full development of our sons' potential—what caring mother *wouldn't* analyze all available statistics and use her own understanding of the game if this approach could bring out the best in her young?

And another thing—Laura and I knew, secretly, that if given the chance, we could out-coach any man at Buckhead. The odds being against our stepping into this role, however, and Coach Jim being well, less than strategically thorough in his approach, we did what we could. Laura's husband, Dave, was Coach Jim's assistant that season, his first mate. Boy, did that come in handy. Dave loved his wife, and Laura wasn't above sweet-talking him into *gently* manipulating Coach's game plan. Thus, by about game six in the Cobras' season, she and I could gaze with pride at the diamond when our boys took the field. Every last player was where he ought to be, in a position he could field with some success.

Deep in our hearts, Laura and I knew we were venturing close to foul territory. We *knew* the point of Little League is to teach the basics of the game, including playing infield, to every player. We *knew* the important thing is for players to learn good sportsmanship and fair play. We *knew* we were breaking nearly every ethic we'd been briefed about early in our careers as tee-ball moms. (*Never* question a coach's strategies, decisions, or overall skills. Or my personal favorite: *never, ever* use whining, disparaging questions in your conversations with other parents.) We may be competitive, Laura and I, but we're not stupid. We *knew,* and thus did we strive to keep our tactical planning sessions covert. We certainly didn't want to adversely affect our young impressionable sons (or their playing time).

But winning was so much fun! And, we reasoned, who enjoys winning more than a nine-year-old boy? Wouldn't bringing home a trophy at season's end make up for certain less-attentive players putting in a little extra time in right field?

◆   ◆   ◆

To open the tournament season, the managed-by-committee Cobras swept by a top-seeded team and from there advanced easily to the tournament's semifinal game, which fell on the 31st of May, an achingly perfect day for baseball, jewel-blue sky the perfect backdrop for the soft green flora of early summer in the South. A ripe, lazy breeze swirled through the park, wafting across the bleachers the scents of popcorn and freshly cut grass. It was hot, but May-hot, not the wretched humid-hot of August. The AA field fairly shimmered, ringed with balloons and banners on each side, navy and silver for the Cobras, the same jewel sky blue and white for our opponents. SINK THE SEA WOLVES, read our banner, primitively sketched in Sharpie marker.

Having bribed my mother to sit with Emma, I watched a few innings of solid defensive baseball in pure contentment. There wasn't much offense, which was no surprise for the Cobra parent. We had won most of our regular-season victories by eking out a few runs and relying on our strong (stacked) infield defense. But the Sea Wolves were deep in offensive talent, or so it had seemed during the regular season. They had often won by wide margins, scores like 18-6, or 22-12. But on this made-for-baseball day, the mighty Sea Wolves looked like sleepy pups, swinging and missing or grounding out on fat pitches.

"Are they missing somebody?" I asked Laura, scrambling for my roster book.

"Don't think so. And JT is here this time."

JT, the Sea Wolves' manager, had been absent from our regular-season game. JT was a nice guy, a devoted father who had enough control over his time to skip away from work at four or five to focus on youth sports. He was coaching his son, Harris, for the fourth year straight and had become a top-notch manager. His laptop computer was hot-wired with all sorts of stats, crammed full of spreadsheets bearing crucial information, updated regularly and carried over from season to season, on just about every player in the league. JT *knew* the game of baseball, and he really liked to win. So you'd think his team would play better with him around.

Through five innings, the score was tied at two. In the top of the sixth, with one out and nobody on, Sam came to bat and hit a weak grounder to the third baseman on the first pitch.

"Aw hell, Sam," I said, loudly enough to be heard by parents close at hand, if not by Sam. Poised by the fence, Houston turned and caught my eye in reprimand. I dropped my head in despair and shame. Then a yell echoed my sentiment from the opposition's dugout.

"Oh hell, Victor, what d'ya think this is, tee-ball?"

It was JT, chiding his third baseman (one of the Sea Wolves' all-stars) a bit too much in the public eye. I glanced at first base and sure enough, Sam was safe. Victor's throw from third had sailed over the first baseman's head.

"All right, Sam! Way to go, bud!" I hollered despite the fact Sam had done nothing more than hustle on a poorly hit ball. I glanced at the on-deck circle—our two heavy hitters were up next. My heart thumped, my mind spinning with all sorts of delicious possibilities. If we could produce a load of runs, we might just survive the Sea Wolves' final offensive threat.

Laura leaned into my shoulder, adrenalin pulsing.

"OK, Charlie, you're a hitter!" she screamed at her son, our next batter. "We can do this, Cobras!"

"Yeah, we can *do* this!" came a shout from the far end of the bleachers. I turned to see none other than Marie the Skeptic, on her feet and clapping. Despite his premature exit from that Opening Day game, her son Joshua was enjoying his best season yet in Little League, and Marie had, let's say, softened her approach. How my heart leapt at her conversion!

The first pitch to Charlie flew wildly out of range of the catcher. By the time the poor child came up with the ball, Sam had stolen second without so much as a slide. From the opposing dugout, JT glared at his pitcher in a way I'd never seen a coach glare before. His face swelled with a live, vicious anger aimed at the little nine-year-old on the mound, a little nine-year-old who also happened to be his son. But JT composed himself, called time, and walked out to the mound to encourage Harris. *Phew,* what a relief—good old JT again.

But Harris walked Charlie. With one out and men on first and second, Stan "the Man" Reynolds came up to bat for the Cobras—Stan, our only true power hitter. *Quelle chance!*

"You're the one, Stan!" intoned Jim from his post as third-base coach. "*Nice, even* swing!"

"You are *the man, Stan*," declared Laura. Our dugout liked the sound of that. Soon the whole place echoed with chants of Stan the kid being Stan the Man.

Harris wound up and threw wild. The ball bounced past the Sea Wolves' catcher, and our runners advanced. We had men now on second and third. Being composed of blood and tissue rather than steel, Harris could not withstand the pressure. In fact, he looked like he might at any moment dissolve into the mound like the Wicked Witch of the West into her puddle. Like any smart coach, JT made a move, motioned to his ace reliever.

As Victor the All-Star took his practice pitches, the noise from our dugout dwindled, then gave way to nervous silence as he painted the corners of the plate with all fifteen fast balls. But our Stan *was* in fact *the man*. After making perfect contact with Victor's first blazing strike, he raced all the way to third while two outfielders fought to retrieve the ball in the left-field corner then tossed it willy-nilly and out of reach of the cutoff man. Down the bleacher, Marie shouted, "Yes! *All the way, Stan!* Home run! Home run!"

"All the way! All the way!" Laura and I chimed in. Yet Stan did not heed us, *nay*, could not heed us. Instead of barreling home as he well should have, he slammed his cleats into the dirt after rounding third, spraying a cloud of red dust over our crystal-clear day. The force of his deceleration was so great his body rose skyward and crashed to the ground. He then rolled over and dragged himself back to third to avoid being tagged out. Beside him on one knee was Coach Jim, his arms thrust stiffly in front of his chest, frozen in baseball's standard stop signal.

"Jeeee-zus! What is he thinking?" Laura asked rhetorically, arms flung wide, just before glancing at the scoreboard, which was being manned that day by a Sea Wolves' parent. "And hey!" she went on, elbowing me, shaking a finger at the board's neon numbers. "A little help, here?" she hollered. It's *four* to two?"

She was right, our last run had yet to be tallied, and the mother, a lovely (clueless) blonde (no doubt the team mom), looked our way, shrugged as her manicured thumb ticked up the run, and smiled sweetly.

I took this as an ill omen.

And Jim's behavior simply did not compute—why had he held Stan at third? He'd certainly neglected to consult with Laura and me on this one. Had he lost track of the ball? Or was this yet another manifestation of his fair-mindedness? Was winning so insignificant, even undesirable, for the parent intent on raising noncompetitive offspring, that we should try to avoid it?

Naaa, fair-minded as he was, Jim did take pride in his team, yet there he stood, smiling and patting Stan on the shoulder as he rubbed his right hip, bruised from the force of his fall. As bewildered as his now silent fans, Stan stood right there, plastered to third base for the rest of the inning, watching dumbfounded with the rest of us as Victor composed himself, struck out our next two batters, and in so doing, regained for his team that most important intangible of youth baseball—the *momentum*.

As the Cobras took the field, we clung to a two-run lead. Laura and I held a collective breath, trying to retain hope, reasoning that, for goodness sakes, they were the ones who should be nervous! Maybe Coach Jim would put in the strong infield we had proposed, and all would be well.

As his infielders tossed the ball around the horn, Sam took the mound. Yes, in the end, all the Cobras' hopes fell on my son, Jim's closer for the day. I felt faint, my mind swarming with visions of Sam doling out consecutive walks and gift wrapping for the Sea Wolves a berth in the AA Championship Game. But Sam's warm-up was strong. Normally rather tentative on the mound, he hurled his pitches with authority and confidence, seeming to be more his father's son on that day than mine. *Momentum shift?* This hadn't registered with Sam—he was full of fire and optimism.

The Sea Wolves' first batter, Billy Baker, swung and missed twice. Our bleachers swelled with renewed hope. Sam, not a strikeout pitcher, was outdoing himself.

"Attaboy, Sam, just throw it by 'em!"

"Here we go, Cobras!" chanted Marie, newly crowned queen of the nonspecific cheer.

"One more strike, Sam!" shouted Laura.

Sam's next pitch *was* a strike, but one Billy managed to make contact with. Luckily, it was not good contact, but an easy ground ball. I sat back with relief and waited for Stan, our all-star second baseman, to chalk up out number one. Instead, Stan pivoted and scrambled into right field in hasty pursuit of the ball, which had slipped under his glove, demonstrating the old lesson that even all-stars are susceptible to momentum shifts.

Billy, also known as "the Roadrunner," sprinted to first base. As the umpire called time, Sam tore at a fingernail with his teeth but held his shoulders back, resisting his little devil of self-doubt. He struck out the next batter, just before that pesky Victor ripped his first fast ball into left field.

Runners were on the corners now with one out. Down at third, little Billy danced pirouettes. JT, coaching third, somehow didn't seem the least bit concerned about Billy getting picked off. In fact, I thought I saw him smirk, then wink—*Yes, he winked at me!* I nudged Laura, but by the time she turned to look, JT was calmly whispering to his runner.

Inhaling deeply, Sam stared down Harris, the new batter. Victor stepped off of first to tie his shoe, and Sam nearly threw over, forgetting time had been called. When play resumed, he turned and glared at Billy, still pirouetting around third.

"Just worry about the batter, Sam!" I yelled. "That guy's not going anywhere!" Which was true in theory. Little League rules forbid base runners from leading off, meaning that once a pitcher comes set to pitch, each runner must have a foot on base and must keep it there until the ball is pitched and crosses home plate. At that point, if the ball gets away from the catcher, or if the pitcher can't control the throw back from his catcher, the runner can steal.

Yet Sam fidgeted. And Billy danced and lunged, his foot somehow stationary on the bag. He and JT (I swear he was smirking at us again) looked so smug, like they didn't care whether Sam ever came set to pitch.

Sam did come set. Wound up and hurled Harris a ball that caught in a gust of wind (at least that's how I like to remember it) and rose high above our catcher's outstretched mitt. Sam's control had betrayed him. JT sent Billy racing for the plate, and Victor ran all the way to third as Sam covered home, to no avail.

The score then was 4-3 with Victor on third and Harris still at the plate. Nearly five minutes had passed since he stepped up to bat, and Sam had thrown him only a single pitch. I crawled off the bleachers and slinked to my old post near the outfield fence, same spot I used to occupy during the previous season to watch Sam strike out to end game after game. Here, the negative karma was not so strong. Here, I could watch Sam's shoulders droop, could nearly feel the damp swipe of his sleeve against his cheek, but he couldn't see me. And the other mothers couldn't hear me gulping away my own tears.

Jim the Fair-Minded called time and met Sam at the third-base line to reassure him, no doubt—"Are you OK? Want me to put in a new pitcher?"

Yes, yes, I thought. *Take him out. Ease his pain.*

But Sam sucked in a breath, dabbed at the corners of his eyes, and shook his tender head. "I want to finish the game," he was surely saying. "Let me get 'em out on my own, Coach. Let's go to the championship!"

Don't listen to him, Jim! He is my little boy!

Thus did my competitive nature shrink in the face of my child's potential failure. Although this moment held the potential for overwhelming success, the kind that could boost a kid's self-esteem for months, things were too intense here. I could feel it, as heavy and dark as the thunderhead that passed briefly over our baseball sun, this burden was too much—for me, if not for Sam. If there was to be glory, let some other deserving player have it.

Jim slapped Sam on the rear before leaving him, alone, on the mound. I blinked, gathered myself, and clapped 'til my palms ached, hoping if I could muster hope, Sam would sense it somehow.

After countless fouled-off pitches, Harris drew a walk. Only he didn't walk, he dropped his bat and ran. As Sam turned away, stomping the rubber in self-disgust, Harris hunkered down and ran like a little fullback, his dad, JT screaming the whole way—

"Take second! Take second!"

Harris rounded first but hesitated. Maybe he'd missed his father's sign. Or was this screaming simply part of some sinister plan? Sam looked over, saw what was up, and snapped to attention. His catcher threw. Sam snared ball in webbing and glared first at Harris, then turned towards third to threaten Victor (now dancing like Billy had), should he try to steal home. This is a standard trick play in the higher leagues: before time has been called after a walk, a coach can send his runner on first to second, thus enticing the pitcher to do the obvious and throw him out while the runner at third sneaks home. Sam was somewhat familiar with the play, but such deceit was rare in the AA league.

Possibly Harris wasn't getting along with his dad. Maybe he wanted to earn a win by benefit of hits, but he didn't seem interested in stealing. A slow runner, he undoubtedly sensed he was a sacrificial lamb. JT wanted nothing more than to *undo* Sam and would gladly chance an out at second in order to tie the game and rely on other hitters (and Sam's vulnerability) to get the winning run. It boiled down to a mental standoff between two nine-year-olds and a thirty-eight-year-old man. As long as the runners threatened to steal, the umpire could not call time.

"Take second!" JT fumed, knees locked, arms stiff at his sides, torso inclined to his frantic son. Harris, still caught in a lunge six feet off first base, was suspended between the disappointment of being thrown out and the prospect of facing his father's wrath later.

But surely Sam would *not* throw to second. He'd have an out at home if Victor ran. But Victor had become an enigma, standing calmly at third as if he wasn't even part of the play.

"Take second. *Now!*"

Finally, Harris submitted. And Sam did the unthinkable. He threw to second. He couldn't resist. Or maybe he decided to trust Victor, believing perhaps that the AA world was a fair place after all. Sam made a clean throw, Stan tagged Harris out, then came up and threw home to try and double up Victor, who by then had already crossed the plate—*safe.*

Tie ball game. As predicted, Sam the boy came undone and could now barely see for his tears. He walked another batter, at which point, too late, Jim brought in some relief. Yet the Sea Wolves' mighty offense had awakened. A couple of hits were all it took them to win the game.

With that, the Cobras' season came to a close. I watched our boys line up to shake hands with their foes and was moved by the calm, mature way they filed past their opponents, shaking hands with even JT, who slapped each Cobra on the shoulder, a sick, haughty grin across his face. I wasn't sure I could look JT in the eye, much less shake his hand. I wasn't sure I would ever feel the same about him again.

For distraction's sake, I began removing our team balloons. Laura walked out to commiserate with me at the fence, offering her condolences and reassuring me that Sam had done as well as could be expected given the situation. Although in the days ahead we would rant about JT and his conniving ways that seemed so out of place on a field full of nine-year-olds, we both sensed that our own lineup manipulations and wished-for plays had taken us precariously close to JT's camp. Having so enjoyed the flush of victory, we'd repressed our stronger maternal instincts and replaced them with lust for a championship trophy.

I wandered to the grassy hillside where Coach Jim liked to gather his players for their post-game pep talks. Sam sat slumped against his bat bag, his tan face streaked with veins of tears and dirt. Keeping my distance so as not to embarrass him, I strained to hear Coach Jim's comments.

"That was a tough one, boys. I'm proud of you, all of you, for keeping your heads up, for believing right to the end. You guys never quit."

I glanced at Sam, who dug with a stick at a loose divot of grass, avoiding eye contact with his coach and teammates.

"And everyone gave it all they had. We got some bad breaks, but what a season."

Jim trailed off, speaking only in generalities, which was his way. He focused on the team effort, singling out no one for either triumph or failure, and gingerly avoiding any specific mention of the opposing team's tactics. I couldn't take my eyes off of Sam, whose thin, folded body seemed to sink deeper into the hillside with every word. He carried the world, the world of AA baseball, *his* world, on his shoulders, and nothing Coach Fair-Minded could say would change the responsibility he felt for having disappointed his team.

The thought suddenly occurred to me that it was all my fault, that Sensitive Sam probably felt how deeply I loved the game and thought he'd let me down, too. I hung my head, and no longer able to abide his feverish digging, went to search for Matt on the playground, leaving Houston to comfort Sam after the team broke up. He was better at it anyway, had a knack for saying something encouraging that was also sincere and fair, whereas I would undoubtedly have gushed the lamest of explanations—*That Victor can sure run!* Or, *You played great, just that one bad inning!*

As I lay awake deep in the night, replaying the game's miscues and feeling haunted by the hangdog look on Sam's face, I clung to the old adage that losing builds character. Sam had proven once again that he was a flesh-and-blood little boy, with years of triumphs and failures ahead of him, and he would be stronger for having lived through this defeat. If only his mother could learn the same lesson.... And yes—*I admit it!*—I fretted over his chances of making the All-Star Tournament Team. The odds had been in his favor all season. Coach Jim had nominated him, but would Sam's dubious decisions and weaker play during the semifinals hurt him? All the AA coaches, the men who would select the all-stars, had been at that game. Would they deduce that Sam wasn't tough enough to be an all-star?

After the championship game a few nights later, these coaches met to select the tournament team. By nine-thirty, I'd begun to sweat—the absence of a phone call would mean Sam had not been selected. The phone finally rang just after ten. I calmly picked up the receiver.

"Martha?"

I knew the voice ... full of brass and confidence, it had to be ...

"This is Pete Brown ..." (perennial manager of the tournament team).

"Hi, Pete!" I tried (and failed) to sound nonchalant.

"Is your All-Star home tonight?"

HEY, NOW, YOU'RE AN ALL-STAR

"First practice, two 'til five Friday," Coach Pete said after a chat with Sam. "And there's a parents' meeting Thursday night."

Three hour practices? *Ouch.* And Thursday was the night of the Cobras' team party, the night Little League parents live for, the night when even the most indifferent managers prepare a little something positive to say about each player. Under a conscientious manager like Jim, the night would be rapturous.

"Uh, that's Sam's team party," I offered. "And Houston's on call."

Pause.

"Well, try to work it out," Pete said, a hint of doubt in his voice—*was this really an All-Star Family?* "One of you needs to be there."

"Oh, sure," I recovered. "No problem! See you Thursday, uhh, um ..." I struggled here—how should one address a man so important in the athletic life of one's child, *Coach Brown? Old buddy? Your Honor?*

"Uh ... see you Thursday, Pete!"

Brilliant.

I hung up in a cold sweat, hands trembling, mind turning back flips to come up with a workable solution. I could leave the other children with a sitter, take Sam to the party and linger until just before the parents' meeting. Or maybe Houston could break away and go to the meeting himself. Might be a slow night in the E.R!

Thus did I fool myself, knowing well the Murphy's Law of On-Call. Having been a medical wife for thirteen years, I knew better than to make leisure plans on nights reserved for healing the sick, yet I bravely hired the sitter and said seven rosaries that Houston's beeper would remain quiet. Sam and I made it to the team party, which according to tradition was held at a Buckhead sports bar (so our pint-sized sluggers could shoot some pool alongside *real* athletes like the softball stars from Al's Tire and Axle). While the kids played video games and tanked up on colas, I munched chicken fingers and mulled over the season's highs and lows with Laura and Marie the (Reformed) Skeptic. Then, just as Coach Jim began to rustle his highly organized and *typed* pages of notes, my cell phone rang. Sure enough, the O.R. awaited, and Houston couldn't make the parents' meeting, which started in five minutes, in a neighborhood fifteen minutes away.

I regretted to Jim that I would miss the best part of his party and motored the family van to the home of—guess who—Mrs. Been There, Done That, whose son Walter was the other all-star traveler to have been elected from the Cobras. Mrs. Been There, also known as Annie McMillan, was of course the team mom, since Walter had been a bona fide all-star the previous season as well. In fact, I found Annie's home thanks to the slightly soiled *B* cap that adorned her mailbox, the mate to the star-studded cap owned by Neighbor Jack that had so confused (and inspired) me on that October day that now seemed so remote. My heart skipped—*my Sam would soon own such a cap!* And it mattered not that he had personally thrown away the Cobras' last chance at glory. The playing field, so to speak, had been leveled anew.

At the hand wave of Walter's churlish, adolescent brother, I dashed to the McMillan basement, where the team meeting was well underway, and squeezed into a child-sized chair next to a card table holding a tray of soggy chips and salsa. Neighbor Jack's mom, Louise, turned and smiled, whether in greeting or in disbelief that I would show up late, it was hard to say.

"So that's why we want to discourage the boys attending any sort of day camp during the all-star season," Pete was saying. "You know, it just drains them so they can't give us that 110 percent we're looking for at practice each night."

Each night? 110 percent? Where and for how long? And what exactly did he mean by *day* camp? Boy, I could see why attendance was mandatory. Surely Pete would applaud the fact that months ago I'd signed Sam and his brother up for a *baseball* camp at a local high school during the first two weeks of June.

"Well, we consider the all-star experience the equal or better of any day camp," Pete explained to some other bewildered parent. "Our boys will get intensive training and much more one-on-one than at any baseball camp."

So that was it. I was supposed to forfeit the 150 cool ones I'd shelled out for this camp. No make that 300, since Matt would never consider going without Sam.

"In fact, we'd like to discourage the boys from playing tennis or going to the pool. You know how hot it gets around here!"

You can say that again, I thought, fanning myself with a cock-tail napkin. Three minutes into the meeting, I was as wilted as day-old spinach.

"You mean on game days?" ventured Susie White, whose son, Hank, was another first-year player like Sam.

"Game days, practice days, we need 'em fresh whenever we get 'em. Now they'll have Saturdays off, of course. Let 'em swim like fish on Saturdays!" Pete chortled.

Susie, trying to chuckle along, whimpered as she sank slowly into her vinyl recliner.

And what will they do all day? she was surely wondering. How in heaven's name is a mother-opposed-to-Nintendo supposed to entertain a nine-year-old boy just out for the summer from sunrise to 6:00 PM for twelve solid days?

"Oh, don't worry," perked up Mrs. Been There. "Walter and the others had a ball last year. We got them together for movies. Pizza parties. It was great!"

Dear God.

I sat, dazed, the chair's edge cutting into my thighs, while Annie handed out rosters and medical releases and reviewed our all-star budget. A debriefing at the Pentagon would seem less complex.

"The league also requires a certified birth certificate for each player," Annie said. "We'll need those by practice on Sunday afternoon."

Sunday—let's see that was one workday away. I rearranged my legs under the snack-laden table, contemplating the last time I'd needed a birth certificate for Sam, when I'd signed him up for tee-ball. Somehow I'd gotten through the first six years of his life without that little certified piece of paper. He was born in Augusta, Georgia, *before* the advent of the Internet, and the red tape involved in getting proof of birth or death from a mere 150 miles away was insurmountable. The tee-ball commissioner had settled for the souvenir certificate the Augusta hospital had issued us after I had it notarized by my attorney-brother. Would the AA Little League gurus go for this?

And I hadn't a clue where that notarized thing was. I had yet to start a *vitae* file for Sam, whose report cards and standardized test scores simply floated in a sea of preschool artwork and papier-mâché in the bowels of my closet. Besides, it wasn't like anyone was going to question Sam's legal age. He was scrawny! Only 45th percentile for a nine-year-old! I glanced around the room. No other mom, not even Susie, looked the least bit worried over the birth certificate issue. They probably knew just where their children's social security cards were, too.

After Walter modeled one of last year's all-star practice jerseys to prove that our money would be well spent, the meeting adjourned.

"I am *so-o-o* glad to have someone to carpool to practices with!" Neighbor Louise gushed. "Jack will *love* having Sam on the team! You know, he was the only one from their class last year."

"I know," I said, fumbling to organize my paperwork. "Was Jack able to handle the practice schedule OK?" I ventured, feeling a surge of empathy for Marie.

"Oh, sure," Louise said. "It's not so bad, really. Just be sure you have plenty of videos on hand. And, oh—Sam will get lots of use out of his Gameboy!"

I smiled and followed her out, wondering if we could afford to buy *three* Gameboys, one for each of the hot, stir-crazy little monsters who would soon be invading my children's bodies.

Getting through the first official practice day wasn't so bad. Sam was too excited about being an all-star to complain about being cooped up in the house. We'd spent the two previous days at the pool, and everyone was parched and needed to purge of chlorine anyway. Still, I was glad for an early dinner, necessary since Sam had to be at practice by 6:00 PM. No, make that 5:45—*Have your all-star there at least fifteen minutes early*, Pete Brown had urged. *We want them loosened up and ready to play before 6:00!*

I prepared macaroni and cheese with smoked sausage and pineapple chunks on the side, Sam's favorite meal, in hopes of inspiring him to make a strong first impression. He inhaled the mac and cheese but hardly touched the other, instead drumming his fingers on the tabletop and kicking the leg of his chair, awaiting permission to be excused. As he cleared his place, I noticed his fingernails were ragged, bitten to the quick. Brave boy, he'd been tearing at them throughout the quiet afternoon, trying to calm his nerves and release pent-up energy while suppressing the urge to terrorize his siblings.

One day, and it had already come to this. I felt justified in having postponed withdrawing the boys from their baseball camp, which started Monday. On Saturday, the cherished swimming day, it rained. Scratch that, it poured. The heavens wept and howled. Although they remained calm as long as a given cartoon played on the TV screen, with each commercial break the kids grew more restless and unruly. By the time *Smurfs* reruns began at 11:30, Emma and Matt could sustain no more of Sam's physical dominance of pillow fights and King of the Couch. I dragged them to the mall food court for lunch.

"What'll it be?" I asked, trying to maneuver Emma's stroller through a throng of Saturday shoppers balancing plates of nachos and milkshakes. "Chinese or burgers and fries?"

"Fries, fries!" chanted Emma.

"Corn dogs!" pleaded Matt. "I want corn dogs!"

"Sam?" I asked, wondering why my firstborn voiced no preference.

"Doesn't matter. I'm not that hungry," he murmured, forgetting the preadolescent notion that consuming junk food has little to do with hunger. *Nerves again.* Fraught with worry, I choked down some fried rice while he pushed bits of corn dog around his plate. A typhoon raging around us, we returned home for Emma's nap by 1:30, the boys drenched and ketchup-stained and ornerier than ever.

"Mom, make Matt sit somewhere *else*," Sam cried from his end of the couch. "He keeps *breathing* on me!"

"He's on *my* side!" Matt answered.

"Why don't you boys go outside and play?" I suggested. "The rain's let up."

"It's too hot."

"We could fill up the baby pool!" I pleaded.

"The water's too cold."

Hmmmm. What was that Annie had said about pizza parties?

◆   ◆   ◆

After Tuesday evening's practice, Sam slouched into the kitchen for something to drink, dusty cleats scuffing the hardwood floors, and I swallowed my usual reprimand about changing shoes in the garage.

"Things OK at practice, bud?"

"Yeah. I guess." He opened the orange-juice carton, tipped it skyward, and swigged away. Again I choked back a nag, snapped away instead at the green beans I was preparing for dinner (another of his favorites).

"The other guys nice?"

"Yes, *Mom*." The refrigerator door rattled and slammed. "They're fine."

And with that, Sam was gone, slouching back to the basement from whence he'd come, a little cloud of despair hanging like a shroud around him, sort of like Pigpen and his ever-present puff of dust. I scooted over to sponge away the smudges of infield dirt he'd left on the refrigerator, wondering what had become of his enthusiasm. Where had gone the bright smile he'd flashed when he found out he was an all-star? Were his coaches coming down too hard on him?

Not at all, said Houston, who deferred to the facts of the matter. Early indications were that Sam would be the team's center fielder, a *critical* position, according to his coaches. But Sam had never before played more than his required inning in the outfield. One of the hardest lessons a developing Little Leaguer has to learn is that not everyone can play the infield forever.

"Strength down the middle wins ball games!" we told Sam, referring to a theory we'd discussed often with reference to pro baseball. But still he slouched, not believing even the adults he trusted most. Against all logic, he concluded he simply wasn't as strong a fielder as his teammates. Surely *that* was why he'd been banished to the outfield.

"You think he's been too worn out at practice?" I later asked Houston, my psyche tainted with secret guilt over having let the boys go to camp after all.

"No, I don't," my confident spouse assured me. "Pete says he's looking great. Quit worrying; it's just baseball practice."

Just baseball practice? Clearly, only a mother could recognize the long-term ramifications of performance in sports for a boy like Sam.

I slept little that night for worrying over whether to keep Sam home from camp the next day. It *had* been hot, ninety-three degrees when I'd picked the boys up on Tuesday. But Wednesday morning dawned overcast with a forecast for drizzle until mid-afternoon. Figuring the camp directors would have the boys doing something indoors, we set out. I dropped the boys off, reassuring them I would be back at noon to take Sam to his team movie (the first organized outing yet). He would be well rested for that night's practice.

As I strapped Emma into her car seat for the trip home, I heard a familiar voice, Annie, chatting with another mom about carpooling on Friday, the last day of camp.

"Hi, Mrs. Payne," said Walter behind me.

Well, well, I thought, relief washing over me. *Mrs. Been There, Done That, team mom and founder of the Quiet Team Activity Club, was a secret rule offender herself! Sly devil, she couldn't resist getting a little extra practice time for Walter.*

I turned smugly.

"Oh, hi, Walter. Sam didn't mention you were in camp with him."

"Oh, I'm not," Walter said smiling, a devious if sleepy glint in his eye. "My brother's here with one of the older age groups. Mom cancelled my place 'cause of all-stars."

I fiddled with Emma's hair, wiped her damp chin with my sleeve.

"Oh, too bad," I stammered. "The boys are having a great time!" I slid into my seat, noticing that indeed Walter wore no tell-tale gear, no cap to calm his bed-rumpled hair, no cleats but rather flip-flops on his oversized feet.

"Mommy, I need my *blanky*!" howled Emma, who at three and a half still felt insecure on the streets without the grungy slip of flannel and satin that had in some other life been a bona fide blanket.

"Bye, Walter!" I called, tossing Emma the blanky and throwing the van into reverse, feigning a rush so as to avoid Annie altogether.

◆ ◆ ◆

As a blistering sun rose on Sam's second week of practice, his siblings and I deserted him. Long before he was elected to the tournament team, we had planned to strike out in mid-June for the Georgia coast where the various members of my extended family would be camped out in a beach house big enough to shelter the Chinese army. This was a tradition my parents cleverly orchestrated to encourage family unity when I was a teenager. Rent a place near sand and sun and pick up the tab. Back then, my five older siblings, all scraping along on starter salaries, couldn't resist dragging their spouses and children from all corners of the country to join us. After we married and had children, Houston and I certainly knew better than to pass up a vacation on the folks, and our kids would scheme for weeks, arguing over who would room with which long-lost cousin and who would catch the biggest wave.

But during that Summer of the All-Star, Sam would enjoy only a couple of days, maybe fewer, with his long-distance relatives. All depended on how the Buckhead Travelers fared in the district tournament. So we arranged for Sam to spend evenings at home with Dad, while days he would hang out with Neighbor Jack and Mom Louise. Sam approved this plan himself, yet who could anticipate the heartache he would feel as his brother and sister and I loaded up our van with boogie boards and buckets?

The van's back side dragging beneath the weight of bikes and fishing gear, we drove around the corner to Jack's. On the doorstep, I hugged Sam tight. He surprised me by hugging me back. Then I kissed his forehead, avoiding the angst of his sad green eyes, and bolted for the car. Driving away, I glimpsed him slowly waving his nine-year-old hand and bit my lip.

"Bye, Sam!" Matt hollered, a note of nostalgia in his six-year-old voice. "Good luck in your games!"

I fixed my gaze on the road, eyes stinging and knuckles bloodless where they gripped the steering wheel. *And I called myself a mother? Trading cherished family time for a little all-star nomination?* I stole a glance in the rearview just in time to see Sam's narrow shoulders give in to that familiar slouch. He seemed suddenly so small, far too young to be left behind for one day with friends, much less four.

Yet on I drove, and on he hit and caught the baseball, securing for himself in those last days of practice the starting position in center field—"Lassie," Coach Pete nicknamed him, in honor of the graceful way he loped across the outfield to chase down soaring fly balls. And he'd made the starting batting order—he was ninth but in there, nevertheless!

Once settled in at the beach, I whiled away the hours policing Matt as he challenged the Georgia surf and brushing sand off of Emma's sunburned thighs. Time spent reconnecting with my siblings offered meager distraction for my maternal obsessions. I slept poorly when I slept at all, worrying not only about Sam missing his vacation but also about how four days with Jack and Louise would affect his sports psyche. Jack was a seasoned competitor, a repeat all-star, not to mention one of those boys who performed as if playing tournament baseball was kind of like brushing your teeth each morning. He fielded at short like Derek Jeter and could seemingly hit blindfolded. I worried his aplomb would intimidate Sam, render him a shivering pulp of nerves.

Saturday, the day Houston would join us, seemed weeks in coming. By the time he arrived, his play-by-play of the last days of practice was overshadowed by the fact that three-year-old Emma had developed a low-grade fever. I began to decompensate—our plan for the second half of the vacation involved Houston's staying at the beach with the little ones while I returned to escort Sam to his first two tournament games. Yet my hyper-mom conscience nagged—should I be the one to nurse Emma? At that age, she was anything but a Daddy's girl. And besides *(ah—here's the rub!)*, would she be well enough by Monday to attend the beach day camp she was signed up for so Daddy could play golf?

We decided to risk it. Those oceanside golf courses are to die for, and Emma's favorite aunt could step in to administer Tylenol and encourage her off to camp. I found I couldn't bear to think of missing Sam's tournament, and, too, Sam had a prior commitment that I felt compelled to be present for—his first date with the orthodontist.

THE BRUSHBACK

For months, Sam's mouth had been secretly under siege by his permanent teeth, all of them pushing their way in at once, invading a space that his genetic map had made too compact to contain such enormous chompers. Something had to be done *and fast*, said his orthodontist. The first stage, *expanding* the workable space in the oral cavity (*yowee*), would require biweekly visits—best to get started during the all-star season so as to have plenty of time to wrench Sam's teeth into place before he left for summer camp in August.

On the afternoon of my return to Atlanta, I phoned the dental assistant.

"Will he be in any pain after his visit tomorrow?" I asked.

"*Pain?*" she replied, seemingly outraged at the very idea. "*Naaa*, nothing a little Advil won't cure. He'll be a little sore, but if he's diligent with his saltwater—rinse and spit, on the hour, every hour! Well then, he should recover Johnny-on-the-spot!"

Hmmmm. I mulled this over. Insert expander at nine-thirty, administer Advil, rinse and spit until, say three, take more

Advil, and like magic, Sam is Johnny-on-the-spot pain free by
five when he must show up for tournament warm-ups.

"Mrs. Payne?" the assistant sputtered. "*Mrs. Payne?*"

"Still thinking!"

To be proactive and change the appointment, thus jeopardiz-
ing full reconstruction of Sam's mouth by the appointed dead-
line? Or to go with the flow and hope sore gums wouldn't
compromise his performance? I needed a second opinion.

"See you at nine-thirty sharp!" I confirmed, knowing if I
called back to cancel within twenty minutes, I could still avoid
being charged for the appointment.

"I think he'll be fine," Houston reassured me in his most
authoritative doctor's voice. "No, a little mouth pain shouldn't
hurt his ability to play.... Yes, I'd go ahead and take him tomorrow.... Oh, yes (*cheery tone*), my golf game was great! ... No, I
don't think Emma went to camp. Is Sam home?"

"You don't *think* she went to camp?" I asked in disbelief.
"Don't you *know* one way or the other? Does she still have
fever?"

"Uh, I left for golf before camp started. And, uh, no, I think
her fever's gone."

"*It's 100.8, Dad!*" Matt in the background, providing an
update.

"Well, she still has a little," Houston recovered. "But she
seems fine now!"

I gritted my teeth then went on in *my* most authoritative
mother's voice.

"What is she doing *now*?"

"She's asleep."

It was 6:30 PM. Emma hadn't gone to bed before eight-thirty
since she was an infant.

"Asleep? For the night?"

"No. Napping."

I rolled my eyes and paced the kitchen, trying to subdue the urge to *control* this situation from three hundred miles away.

"OK. Well. I hope she sleeps tonight!" I said, secretly wishing she'd have him up in the wee hours and show him a thing or two about the importance of a schedule.

"And I guess I'll go on and get Sam's teeth done tomorrow."

"Yes! Do that!" he said. "And enjoy your free time!"

Free time? Was I intended to have free time? Tomorrow, the orthodontist; the next day, batting practice in a neighbor's cage; Friday, I would chaperone the team to a pregame movie. Total free time for the week thus computed to about an hour and ten minutes, not counting laundry and dishes.

◆   ◆   ◆

As luck would have it, the Buckhead Boys of Summer drew as their first tournament opponent their then archrivals, the team from the North Fulton Youth Organization (NFYO), a Little League park just a ten-minute drive from our own. NFYO served players from neighborhoods slightly north and east of Buckhead's Little League domain, but the borders of the two leagues were fuzzy—players sometimes *crossed over* from NFYO to Buckhead or vice versa, usually because of coaching issues. In the 1990s, the two leagues had different philosophies, a difference summed up nicely by the bumper stickers each league produced. The Buckhead sticker read simply BUCKHEAD BASEBALL and was adorned with an endearing caricature of Henry Irby's buck's head. The NFYO sticker, on the other hand, read NFYO diagonally across one end, with BASEBALL in large print just next to it. The word *REAL*, scripted in smaller letters yet not so small as to be missed by anyone with, say, 20/80 vision, was tucked in between NFYO and BASEBALL. The complete message then read NFYO, *REAL BASEBALL*. You get the picture.

When Sam was in Little League, parents of boys who left NFYO for Buckhead generally claimed the NFYO coaches were a little too intense, while those who favored NFYO over Buckhead said they were looking for a more competitive league. Their coaches were often past college players or at the very least, young, eager competitors who played to *win*. Not only that, NFYO's 1998 Nine-Year-Old Tournament Team had Chuck Mitchell, alias "the Flame Thrower." A good four inches taller than any of our boys, Chuck's arm and bat had already become the stuff of legend.

Control. That's what puts that boy head and shoulders above any of our pitchers, Buckhead coaches would lament. *Control and speed …*

Size! That's what sets Chuck apart…. Has anyone checked this kid's birth certificate?

That boy's got talent—I mean talent! Could be headed for the Big Leagues.

"Mom, he thows, like, sixthy mileth an hour," Sam garbled as we traveled across town to Murphey-Candler Park, site of the district tournament. At the orthodontist's office, his size-seven mouth had been stretched and prodded into accommodating lengths of metal set at just the right angle to insure that his man-sized teeth would soon stand up straight and tall. Of course, all the saltwater in Utah couldn't have relieved his swelling by game time. And the Advil? It made him drowsy and distracted. Even so, the fastest nine-year-old pitchers are lucky to clock *fifty* miles per hour, but was there any way to convince Sam of this? Why would he listen to his mother rather than his almighty coaches?

"Just keep your eye on the ball, buddy," I lamely suggested—*how many times had he heard that one?* "You're a good hitter, and I bet your coaches are exaggerating to psyche you guys up."

"Yeah, right," Sam snapped, opening his window. Cap in his lap, he leaned out, the wind in his hair, and spat a glob of blood into the sultry evening air.

A few moments later, we pulled into a parking place.

"Lemme see your mouth again," I said.

"Mom," Sam said, gathering his bat bag. "It'th fine."

"Just let me *see* it, Sam."

With a scowl worthy of a full-fledged teen, he opened his lips and lifted his puffy tongue. Inside the perimeter of his lower teeth lay what looked like an unfurled paper clip, its tips embedded in his gums, red and raw and adorned on each side with a bubble of blood.

I shuddered, swallowed.

"Oh, buddy. I'm so sorry."

"It'th OK, Mom," he said, his eyes softening and filling, much like my own. "It doethn't hurt that bad. I think the Advil ith really tharting to work."

With that, he stood, straightened his team belt, and lifted his bat bag, his personalized all-star bat bag, over his shoulder.

"OK. Good luck," I urged, voice wavering.

And with hardly a wince, Sam managed a swollen, boyish grin. For a brief moment, he posed before me, red Buckhead jersey shining bright and clean and cleats smelling of new leather. Before he walked off, the sun glinted off of his cap, his fitted navy cap embroidered with a regal red *B* and encircled with silver stars.

I turned away, wiped a cheek. At that moment, anything, even literally pulling victory from the bloody jaws of defeat, seemed possible.

Yet by the top of the third inning, Buckhead trailed NFYO, 1-0. Chuck Mitchell dominated from the mound, where he struck a figure every bit as threatening as prophesied. Not only did he have the same lean, long-legged sort of body that David Justice must have had as a nine-year-old, but he'd developed a classic pitcher's glare, one made all the more menacing by the two black swooshes accenting his high cheekbones. He glared, like a Mohawk warrior ready for battle.

The swooshes were nothing more than eye black, which the NFYO team mom had had the foresight to paint on her players during warm-ups to tone down the effects of the summer sun. Angry and blinding in the western sky, this sun seemed to hover behind center field an inch or two above eye level, as if the earth on this heavy, humid day had actually paused on its axis in honor of our game. Not to be outdone, Annie, our own team mom (feeling some pressure on her been there, done that status) scuttled over to the nearest sporting goods store to make a purchase during warm-ups. By the time Sam came to bat for the first time in this third inning, the Buckhead players sported eye black of their own.

With one man on by virtue of a walk and one man out, my little warrior stood in at the plate. Chuck's first fastball blazed near. Sam took a tiny step back with his front foot and swung wildly out of range of the pitch. He spun in dejection, knowing an all-star's gravest sin is to step out and show fear of being hit by the ball, no matter how hard the pitcher throws. Cowering, he turned towards the dugout to read Coach Pete's signal.

Next pitch, he flinched then bravely took a ball over the outside corner. On the third pitch, Sam actually turned towards Chuck, leaning in over home plate. I fretted—*Was it safe for him to bare his chest to The Flame Thrower?* But Sam was squaring to bunt. He lay the ball down a few feet out and to the left of home plate, then took off for first like a young greyhound. The catcher scrambled for the ball and threw to first but not in time for the out. The runner advanced, and we had men on first and second.

"Great job, Lassie!" shouted Susie White, whose son Hank was still on the bench. I turned and smiled in thanks, trying to quell the twinge of embarrassment I felt since only Sam, the number nine batter, had been asked to bunt to advance the runner rather than swinging away. But as fate would have it, the next two batters, top of our lineup, got hits and two runs came in to score, Sam racing across the plate with the go-ahead run. I quickly reevaluated Pete's decision, deciding he was a pretty doggone good manager after all.

As Sam high-fived his teammates in the dugout then turned to give me the slightest and most lopsided of grins, I noticed his eye black had smeared across his nose and begun to drip in little sweat rivulets down his chin. Had Mrs. Been There settled for a budget brand? A glance at Neighbor Jack revealed a similar smudging. In fact, every last Buckhead player sported a sort of tearful clown look, whereas the boys from NFYO retained their solid swoosh of war paint through all manner of sweating and sliding and wiping of cheeks. Apparently, *their* eye black wasn't eye black at all but instead a strip of black fabric, felt or something-like, adhered to the cheek. Well, Annie had done her best.

As the Buckhead Boys headed into their last at-bat, we trailed 3-2. The mood on our bleachers was high, however, since no one had expected us to muster much offense against Chuck. Now, a rally seemed possible. I bit my nails and cheered as our first two batters, cheeks bathed in charcoal gray, reached base on an error and a hit. Nervous energy sizzled among the parents, even the most lackadaisical of whom rose from the bleachers to pace behind home plate or holler encouragement from the fence. The team mood deflated only slightly when Jack, our number seven batter, struck out. His mother, Neighbor Louise, held fast to her enthusiasm for a comeback though her eyes took on that sheepish, apologetic look of the mother whose son has disappointed his team. I, on the other hand, began to feel faint and lightheaded as Jack caught air on his last swing. Sam would now be on deck, and I found myself in that most miserable of Little League parental situations—my son had every chance of making the *last out* of the ball game. If the number eight batter were to record an out, Sam would come to bat with two men on and two men out.

But thank God, number eight got a base on balls. *Maybe the Flame Thrower has lost his control!* I thought. If so, and if he walked Sam, too, the tying run would cross the plate and Sam would be a hero—a passive hero perhaps, but the batter gets credit for an RBI if he reaches base on a walk. I clenched my hands together and prayed for such a cowardly accomplishment, knowing Houston would be disappointed in me—"You gotta believe!" I could almost hear him saying. And it's not that I didn't believe in Sam's potential—it was more a feeling of impending doom, the sort that has raised its ugly head in this sort of high-intensity situation throughout my life. Maybe I got too little oxygen in the birth canal, but when the pressure's on, I tend to anticipate the worst-case scenario. Plus, that fireball of a Georgia June sun had dropped just enough that it shone full on the batter's face while leaving the infield in shadows.

Sam sauntered to the plate, shoulders straight and strong, seeming to sense that Chuck had tired since his last at-bat. He tapped one cleat with the barrel of his bat, turned, eyed the catcher, and spat blood in the dirt, perhaps a little too close to the catcher's foot.

These pitches better be good, he implied. *No bailing out this time, buddy!*

I, however, was harder to convince and would have preferred to avoid this situation altogether. *Think bunt, think bunt*, I recited to myself, reversing my prior wish that Coach Pete let Sam swing for the fences. A good bunt could score a run!

But Sam swung, pretty much for the fences, and missed (*blasted sun!*). Strike one. Sam wiped his chin, where a trickle of blood had mingled with a smear of eye black. Undaunted, he stood in again. On the next pitch, he made contact, and the man on third raced towards home. As Sam hustled up the first-base line, the ball bounced by the pitcher then skidded off the edge of the mound, caroming directly towards the charging NFYO shortstop. Irony of ironies, Sam had hit the ball too hard, too fast, in light of its glancing blow off the mound. The shortstop managed to scoop it up and throw home in one graceful movement, just in time for the catcher to make the tag. A lesser-hit ball, e.g., *a bunted ball*, might have rolled just so on the grass, thus giving the runner time to score before anyone could field it.

Sam was safe at first, but there were now two outs, and we still trailed by one. Chuck tugged at his cap, breathed deeply. Perhaps he found new life in this Ozzie Smithesque play, or maybe he remembered what was what—*Hey, I'm The Flame Thrower man, and you guys are just the boys from Buckhead!* Whatever the case, he recovered his old form and threw three strikes right by Walter, our leadoff hitter.

Sam lingered on first as his teammates retreated to the dug-out. I could almost hear the little voice in his head—*It's my fault. If only I'd hit the ball in the air, or up the middle, or, or, anywhere other than there, we'd be tied right now.* As I fretted over how to console him, a voice boomed behind me:

"Don't you worry—that little slugger will get it next time."

I didn't recognize the voice at first, not until I felt the thud of a heavy hand between my shoulder blades. It was Gus, the shoulder-slapping dad, the one who was so careful to remind me throughout Sam's ill-fated Rookie season that he would, one day, recover his ability to hit a baseball. He was right, not that I needed reminding, then or now. What in the blazes was Gus doing at an all-star game? And what was that on his head—an NFYO cap?

"Yeah, Sammy's come a long way in a couple of years," he continued. "Sort of like my little Gus."

Big Gus winked and nodded, and sure enough, there was the once-mediocre Gus Junior, slouched in the NFYO dugout, wearing a wide grin across his neatly swooshed face.

"We moved him over here this season, and it's made all the difference!"

Ahhh—wanted a more competitive *league, no doubt.*

Gus Junior smiled and stood to shake hands with his coach. No wonder I hadn't recognized him. He'd become a giant of his former Buckhead self—taller, yes, but also ropey and muscular, like his dad. Did they have these NFYO guys lifting weights? Or worse, taking steroids?

"I, uh … didn't recognize him," I said.

"Nobody does!" Gus broke in. "Chip off the old block now! And this program over here has—"

"Gus!" rang out a call from the far bleachers.

"Uh, gotta go!" Gus shouted, trotting away. "You take care and give Sammy my best!"

With that he was gone. *And the "program over here" has what, Gus?* I longed to hear his punch line, to learn the secret of the NFYO machine. I pondered for a moment the possible transformation Sam might have if I managed to switch him to NFYO. Could his baseball future be reconfigured by their young, energetic coaches? Was this the key we'd been searching for, the way to unlock his true potential?

In *their* dugout, Sam and his buddies laughed and shoved each other good naturedly. Walter poured Gatorade over Sam's head, and Sam returned the favor. Soon the place erupted in hysteria, with coaches and players alike hollering, soaked through with sticky fructose. Their defeat forgotten, they were little boys again, buddies one and all.

Cancel that plan for switching leagues. At least he didn't make the *last* out.

◆   ◆   ◆

The Buckhead All-Stars fared better in their next game, and in their fourth, they pulled out a late-inning victory against an impressive Murphey-Candler team. This gave them the edge they needed to reach the tournament's Final Four. If we could win the semifinal round, we might face NFYO in the championship, thereby earning the chance to prove who the real men were in our neck of the woods. However, having reached the semifinals by only that edge, we were doomed to play the number-one seed. The result was about what you'd expect—Bad Guys 9, Buckhead 1. Sam seemed to forget how to hit altogether, and I took to watching from a distance. Squatting on a grassy hillside near the right-field fence, I couldn't see so clearly the shadow of doubt that had settled across his face.

Houston and Matt returned from the beach for these last games. In the heat of the day on the final Saturday of the tournament, Sam and his team played in a consolation game to determine which of the losers from the semis would finish third. Many of Buckhead's players may have actually slept through this game, including Sam, who no longer could blame his teeth for his woes. All the swelling having subsided, he let an easy fly ball fall at his feet then struck out twice, right in front of his older cousin who'd driven into town to see him play—the cousin, that is, who was a star shortstop on her high school softball team.

"Good game," this cousin lied as Sam came off the field.

"Thanks," Sam said, grinning in spite of himself, his expander a-glint in the sun.

"Mom, can we leave straight from here?"

For the beach, he meant. And we did, tucked cleats and bat bag behind the surf-fishing rod and tackle box and were off. The bat bag stayed put, collecting sand and salt spray, until we returned home. Throughout that vacation, Houston and I rehashed the tournament and analyzed Sam's performance ad nauseam. More precisely, I rehashed, and he listened patiently between golf games and riding waves with the boys. I spent lots of time ruminating alongside the baby pool while a now-healthy Emma splashed and giggled. I couldn't erase the image of Sam's brave, bloodied face after he grounded out against NFYO, couldn't shake the feeling that yet again, I had somehow failed him, failed as a mother.

Was it coincidence, then, that during the next few weeks our baseball insurance policy was conceived? Who knew? And no matter. In approximately nine months, perhaps even in time for the next Opening Day, I would give birth to James Ian Payne, our third chance at Little League glory.

TEAM MOM TO BE

By the next February, I'd survived morning sickness and one final ritual reorganization of my abdominal organs in preparation for the waning months of pregnancy. Like his brothers before him, Ian grew very large in utero and enjoyed stretching outward with violent jabs of limb and head, reaching for inclusion in the outside world so that my midsection preceded the rest of me by a good two feet. Consider the backaches, and I hardly need mention the indigestion, irregularity, sleeplessness, swollen digits—standard fare for the expectant mother.

Longing for some sort of inspiration, I waited for that nesting urge to hit. But I was just tired. Well into month nine, the nursery remained set up as my office. The infant seats and bottles, even the bassinet, lay hidden beneath a clutter of hockey sticks and tennis rackets in the basement. Finally, on a random day in mid-March (a mere three weeks prior to my due date), I hobbled down and began easing out boxes of infant nighties and T-shirts, all of which sported significant spit-up stains and reeked of mildew. It was too exhausting for words. Naturally, then, my mind insisted on wandering to other, perhaps less pressing but still crucial issues, such as Sam's upcoming season.

I worried that in my present state I could hardly bend over to pick up a tennis ball, much less pitch to him. Odd, too, was the fact that no one had yet volunteered to serve as team mom for Sam's AAA team, the Red Bugs. We had an unusually organized coach—he'd sent out schedules as well as a written packet (*ten pages, typed, tiny point size*) full of hitting techniques and suggestions for the boys to study (which, of course, few of them did). Maybe he doubled as team parent himself?

No, I soon discovered via Ma Bell, he did not.

"Well, I've asked Rob's mom to help, but she works, you know. As does Mrs. Martin," he began, his voice sort of dim and wilting. "And Spencer's mom is willing, but she's chairing a fund-raising campaign at the middle school."

Certainly wouldn't want to crowd her schedule!

"What about the team mom meeting?" I asked.

"Oh, I stopped by there—"

He stopped by a meeting run by a bunch of homemakers? At midmorning on a weekday?

"And picked up all the paperwork."

A very—ahem—pregnant pause.

"Of course, Opening Day is this Saturday. I, uh," his voice brightened. "I hated to ask you—for obvious reasons!"

And yet, you are.

"But—"

"The baby's due in three weeks," I reminded him, not that I thought it would make any difference.

"Yes, well …"

Another pause, less pregnant.

"Well, we do have that exact week off for spring break," he said.

How serendipitous!

"And I know the other moms will pitch in!"

And just like that, it was done. Elected team mom when I ought to be ironing day gowns and knitting booties. Ah well, I never knitted a stitch for my first three, anyway, and after all, I reminded myself, I was, in fact, the misguided person who'd conceived this child in part to enrich our Little League lives. Team mom at nine months pregnant—how totally appropriate!

"OK!" Such animation now. "Our first game is Saturday at one. You might call and remind the boys to be out at the ceremonies by 9:45, then we'll go on to hit in the cages at 11:00, and maybe grab some lunch before we take infield."

"Sure."

"And one other thing. I plan to keep pretty close stats on these games, and I like to use a reward system. Could you pick me up about, oh, a hundred and fifty of those little yellow stars for their caps? The iron-on type will do fine."

"*Yellow stars?*"

"Take a look at the Major Pirates' caps on Saturday. The guys with the most stars are the toughest competitors."

Whoa, what happened to candy treats and a pat on the back?

"Uh, OK."

"I'm sure you can find the stars at any craft shop."

No problem. If I could manage to hoist my body in and out of the car, I'd nab a couple hundred when I stopped in for a pair of knitting needles.

◆ ◆ ◆

And so Opening Day approached even as Baby Payne number four grew bulbous and heavy. Sam was ten and a half, on the downhill side of fourth grade. As a Red Bug, he was beginning his fifth full season of organized baseball and for the first time would be playing on a team that included not a single one of his close friends. A pitfall of youth sports: the higher a player climbs in the ranks, the more he engages in an athletic endeavor rather than a game played for fun. A couple of Sam's buddies had decided to quit baseball, and the ones still playing had been drafted by other coaches, coaches who more than ever had winning as a goal.

Independent of baseball, since the fall, Sam had been drifting away from some of the boys he used to hang out with (all of whom were polite, adult-friendly, and well-behaved) and homing in on a couple of new ones who hadn't passed my maternal approval test yet, boys who seemed more sophisticated somehow, more socially advanced than his former best buddies. Whereas many of Sam's pre-ten-year-old friends had been innocent and responsible oldest children, all the boys Sam fixated on during his eleventh year on earth seemed to be a ways down in their families' birth order, which meant each was sharing his home with at least one *teenager*. These younger siblings had been exposed, shall we say, to all sorts of influences Sam had to date been immune to. His world had revolved around sports, school, and family. He loved life and liked pleasing his parents.

Yet suddenly, in the company of his new friends, he was confronted with such distractions as PG-13 movies, pyromania, and *girls*.

"Mom, can I go over to Jack's?" he shouted one afternoon for the fourth day in a row after slamming through the door and ditching his backpack in the front hallway. I glanced out the window. Weary and goggle-eyed, Matt, a lowly first grader, struggled off the bus alone, scraping his backpack along the driveway behind him.

"What about your homework?" I asked Sam.

"Did it all," he said, halfway to the kitchen in search of a snack. "On the bus."

"You did it *all?*" I called, lowering my swollen belly, crouching atop shaky knees to greet Matt, red cheeked and dazed. "How was your day, honey?"

"It was OK, Mommy," Matt answered, hugging my neck so hard he nearly tipped me over. Then he drew back. "Can I *please* go with Sam?" he pleaded, eyes large with longing. Though I doubt he knew where Sam wanted to go, he sensed escape was on his mind.

"No, he *can't*." Sam spurted, bolting out of the kitchen, a bag of chips and a couple of juice boxes spilling out of his skinny arms. "See you later, Mom," he continued as he ran through the door which had yet to close from his original entrance.

"Wait just a minute!" I bellowed. Sam did a graceful corkscrew on the front walk.

"Mom, you can check my planner," he said, eyes rolling. "I did it all."

"Mommy, *please*. I can go with Sam, right?" Matt continued, tugging on my shirtsleeve. Sam glared at Matt over his loot.

"And what are you doing at Jack's house? Will his mom be home?"

"I dunno. *Somebody's* there, 'cause Jack got off the bus. Maybe Pete."

Which was exactly what I was worried about. Jack's mother, Neighbor Louise (who was a neighbor in the sense of living in the same subdivision, not next door) was a fun, laid-back mom who was sometimes gone for entire afternoons carting around her older children. Jack often hung out with friends on the block, or worse, stayed with one of his teenaged siblings (i.e., Pete). Now that I have a combination of little ones at home and teenagers with endless afternoon commitments, this plan strikes me as perfectly logical. When my oldest was a mere ten, however, I was a tad uncomfortable with the idea of him running around unsupervised, or worse, slipping into the clutches of some rebellious fourteen-year-old. After Sam attended a recent sleepover at Jack's, I'd discovered in the pocket of his shorts a handful of ash-tipped matchstick nubs along with two firecrackers and a couple of melted army men.

"Sam," I said in my firmest disciplinarian voice. "I *do not* want you playing with matches."

"OK, Mom. I *promise*," he said, smiling now, his green eyes clear and guileless. He hesitated, then dropped his snacks and trotted back to wrap his arms around me in a carefully timed hug, a sideways hug so as to avoid touching my belly button, which had by this point begun to turn inside out and protrude under the thinning fabric of my well-used maternity wear.

"We'll probably just watch a video or something anyway," he added.

Wonderful, I thought. *Lethal Weapon 2, perhaps?*

"I wanna go," Matt whined.

"Sorry, Matt," Sam said, collecting his junk food and prancing up the street, hopping from asphalt to grassy fringe then back again.

"Oh!" I called after him, my pregnancy-challenged scheduling mechanism finally kicking in. "You have practice at five!"

"Aaaww, Mom," he said. "Do I have to go?"

Did he have to go to practice for baseball, his favorite sport?

"Of course you have to go," I said, flabbergasted.

"Do I have practice, Mommy?" Matt asked, eyes brightening. I shook my head. Tee-ball practice, he meant, bless his heart. He ached for a nugget of action in the lonely, Sam-deficient afternoon looming ahead.

"Oh, OK, Mom," Sam relented. "I'll be home by 4:30."

"Call me when you get there!"

"Sure!" he said, racing now beside that grassy fringe, the freedom of a full afternoon having been curtailed.

Of course, come 4:30, I had to hunt Sam down on Jack's cul-de-sac. Though he attended practice faithfully during the early days of that season, there was a new edge to his attitude, a certain impatience with baseball, with me, with life as he had always known it. Was it his confidence that had taken such a hit during that mediocre all-star season? Or could this be a foreshadowing of adolescent torment to come? Was he simply growing away from me, resisting as a matter of course a path his mother seemed to have chosen for him? *(Had I?)*

Maybe. Probably. The truth was Sam seemed always to want to be somewhere *else*, roaming the neighborhood with Jack and other friends, maybe slouched on the sofa in front of the television. Or—here was a new one—seized with computer rapture, his fingers frantically banging the keyboard.

"What you working on?" I asked one warm, sunny Sunday afternoon, the kind of lazy spring day when during his previous life all sorts of enticing activities would have beckoned him outdoors. In fact, Emma and Matt had dug into their drawers and stretched out last year's swimsuits just enough to fit. Just there, through that window above the computer desk, they giggled and shivered, racing each other across the grass as the sprinkler swept across their goose-pimply bodies.

"Nothing," Sam murmured, clicking a window closed.

"Do you have a school project?"

"No, Mom. I told you, it's nothing."

"Well, it can't be nothing."

"It's IM. I'm just IM-ing with Jack."

"*IM-ing?*" I asked. It was only 1998, and the Internet was still a relatively safe place. Yet IM-ing sounded lurid, forbidden.

"It's like talking on the phone, only on the computer."

He expended a heavy sigh.

"Oh," I said, my mind buzzing with questions. I settled for asking if this new form of communication—*Instant Messaging*—was peculiar to him and Jack.

"*Mo-o-om.* Everybody does it."

"You mean like grown-up everybodies, or just kids?"

"How should I know? Everybody at school does it."

As I pondered a tactful way to ask whether females were involved, the computer emitted a melodious string of bells and a little box popped up on the screen. Before Sam could close it, I caught sight of the sender's screen name: HOT-QT.

Well, that saved my asking, anyway.

◆   ◆   ◆

Despite the temperance of Sam's passion for baseball, he overcame his confidence issues at the plate and hit well during his AAA season. As his typed packet of hitting tips should have hinted early on, Coach Yellow Star was obsessed with offense. He'd been careful to draft strong hitters (without paying a dot of attention to their ability to field) and apparently hoped they could absorb the ability to pitch and throw and catch well enough to win ball games.

Alas, they didn't. Maybe it was due to the nasty blisters the Red Bugs developed on their hands while taking the zillions of swings in the batting cage required of them, but no matter how many runs we managed to tally in a game (one particular score of 19-17 comes to mind), we rarely pulled out victories. When Sam pitched, we had a strong fielder at shortstop and another capable defensive player at catcher, and that was about it, which presented Sam with the odd challenge of either forcing batters to hit balls only in the direction of short, or striking them out. If a batter hit a ball, say, weakly towards second base (or first or third), even if it was the softest of grounders, it would inevitably roll a centimeter or two under or over the outstretched glove of our brave Red Bug and on into the outfield. And pop-ups, well, for our foes, the lowly pop-up was destined to become a hit—a double or triple, mind you—if it happened to drop anywhere other than within a six-foot radius of shortstop. Perhaps in retrospect I am too harsh—surely now and then a pop-up or fly ball did, by some act of God, find its way into one of our player's gloves, yet we parents quickly discovered that the sweet spots of those gloves came specially equipped with a jack-in-the-box mechanism that seemed to activate at the exact moment ball plocked leather.

Sadly, rather than a strikeout pitcher, Sam was more of a pint-sized Tom Glavine, a devious lefty who could make the ball dance. Batters often could hit his pitches, slow as they were, without hitting them well. Sam's ability to force outs then depended absolutely on his teammates' ability to field these poorly hit balls. Needless to say, he gave up numerous runs because of fielding errors. Our other top pitcher was in fact that agile shortstop. This presented Coach Yellow Star with a real conundrum—*who was to play short when his one strong infielder pitched?* Finding his options limited and not wanting to waste precious batting time on *training* anyone to field, he began using Sam at short. Problem: as noted, Sam is a lefty! Whoever heard of a left-handed shortstop? Though he tried his best, it often wasn't pretty.

So Sam at short was doomed to bobble and throw wild with the best of his pals, and when he pitched, those pals returned the favor. He became so anxious he finally developed a debilitating tic, a sort of tremor of the left wrist, while on the field or the mound. No surprise then, that Coach Yellow Star quit using him to pitch except in the most desperate situations. And actually, the less frequently Coach called on Sam to pitch, the higher his *hitting* stats climbed. He earned nary a yellow star for defense of any kind *(who did?)* but began adorning his cap with row after row of stars for multiple-hit games or extra base hits. By midseason, he was inching towards the honor of highest batting average on the team.

One Wednesday afternoon, he jumped up from his computer screen to ask if we could leave early for practice, a request that shocked me in light of his budding friendship with Jack, Prince of Preteen Indifference.

"Why?" I asked, checking the family schedule to see if I'd forgotten a piano lesson he was hoping to skip. Why else would the new Sam have donned his baseball clothes and gear without a reminder?

"I just *like* practice on Wednesdays," he murmured, fingering a ball with his left hand while leaning over to type one last message with his right.

"What happens on Wednesdays?"

"I don't know … *nothing*, Mom. Can we go now, *please?*"

Then it hit me. Wednesday was stat day, the day Sam came home from practice clutching in his hot little hand two pages crowded with columns and columns of tedious information. Don't get me wrong—I love a good baseball stat sheet. The apparent predictability of the game, although comforting somehow, is often in such fantastic contrast with how the games turn out. It's sort of like, well, *life*, and I, for one, can't resist studying stats over my morning cereal. And that goes for stats provided by a numbers-happy Little League coach as well as those published in the sports pages.

Coach Yellow Star did not skimp. The Red Bugs were provided with everything from the most basic—BA and RBI for *batting average* and *runs batted in*—to the hopelessly obscure—CRSP, or *contact made with runners in scoring position.* Sam, a born mathematician, also enjoyed poring over these stat sheets, particularly as his BA and perhaps more importantly, his HRSP (*hits* with runners in scoring position) steadily climbed.

Many of the Red Bugs, and some of their parents, hardly bothered trying to decipher Coach's abbreviated headings. Yet with merely a glance at the stat sheet, every one of them could determine the meaning of a paltry, subhundred number by a player's name. Thus, some of Sam's weaker teammates had a vastly different reaction to the stat sheets than Sam did. Since they had no opportunity to excel at defense either, they lost all confidence and fell into Little League funks.

In my tender condition, I suffered great emotional instability throughout this AAA season. On the one hand, elated by Sam's batting achievements (and hopeful his attitude issues would resolve themselves), I sewed frantically, my fingertips growing pricked and sore, to attach his yellow stars between games. (The iron-on method only resulted in a star-littered field by the third inning). And as team mom, I was obligated to demonstrate some show of support for Coach Yellow Star. Yet I ached for Sam's teammates—boys with true potential!—whose numbers slipped lower and lower even as their smiles faded.

By the end of March, I'd grown so large and weary with child that once I completed whatever chores were absolutely required of me, I did little other than sit and fret anyway. I'd reached that most irrational final period of pregnancy when a mother can become so anxious and sleep deprived and uncomfortable that it seems the actual birth will never come. *I will be the first woman in history to simply burst open rather than delivering*, I remember concluding several times over. I'd been having contractions for weeks, I could feel the baby descending by the moment, arms and legs and various other anatomical parts thrashing for release, yet it seemed he or she would never arrive.

My due date came on a Friday, Good Friday in fact, a day when lots of people worry and hurt with all sorts of unpleasant emotions. Most anyone who has been exposed to the Christian faith can't help but feel at least a little *guilt* in particular on Good Friday. Having been raised a Roman Catholic, I am familiar with guilt in all its manifestations. In fact, since reaching adulthood, I've had to labor mightily against a tendency to wallow in guilt over past misdeeds rather than taking charge and actually feeding the homeless or visiting the elderly. But during Lent, I allow myself to go ahead and get as much useless guilt out of my system as possible. Good Friday can be so comforting, a day when everyone—even the cheery, hands-on Episcopalians whose ranks I have joined as an adult—feels sadness and guilt.

So there I sat in my mess of a bedroom while the children played, worrying over everything from not having taken a meal to that neighbor in need in January, to not telling Coach Yellow Star a thing or two about his incentive program. With tearful, prenatal pride, I was stitching onto Sam's cap his ninth yellow star while feeling increasing remorse for his new buddy, Rob, who had only two, when a pang of anguish reached hot and deep inside me. I gasped for breath. *Could it be that our incipient Ted Williams was on deck?* What luck! Our Little League spring break had just begun—I might even give birth and recoup without missing a single game!

An hour or so after midnight, stronger labor pains came hard and fast, and Houston and I headed for the hospital. By the time they wheeled me into delivery, I felt so limp and drained I announced that I'd rather not have this baby at all, that being turgid as a tick for the rest of my life was just fine with me.

"Where the *hell* is the anesthesiologist?" screamed the mad woman inside.

"On the way!" a brave Houston replied.

"Here I am!" called Dr. Angst Relief himself as he hustled through the door.

"About time!" I jeered and rolled over, flooded with that peculiar maternal desire to have someone, *anyone*, jab a syringe into my spine.

Thoughtless of the minimal time required for my epidural to take full effect, James Ian gushed into the world a half an hour later, at 4:07 AM on Holy Saturday. (Probably better for my Catholic tendencies that he waited a few hours after Good Friday.)

"It's a boy!" cried my OB, confirming what I'd sensed all along. Houston glowed—another son, such virility!

Sloppy and red, Ian kicked and screamed like none of his siblings before him. *He's perfect*, I thought in a haze of frenzied exhaustion. Not only beautiful but full of grit and hustle! Eight days later, on the Sunday afternoon before school and Little League would resume the next day, Coach Yellow Star called about setting up an extra batting practice.

"I want to get the boys back on track. We should be winning more ball games than we have been …"

Helps if you teach 'em to catch the ball, Coach.

"Our bats are bound to heat up here now that the weather's improving!"

"I'm sure the boys will do fine," I deferred, trying to cradle the phone on my shoulder and rearrange Ian so his little head would not roll off my arm as I nursed him.

"So, if you could just give everybody a call."

Just then, Emma came howling into the room. Matt had kidnapped her favorite baby doll and hung it just above the toilet in their bathroom. In her rush to rescue Baby Kelly, Emma had slipped and bumped her cheek on the tub, knocking poor Kelly in for an unexpected swim. After sternly ordering Matt to rescue Kelly, I leaned over to pull Emma's hair away from her face and in so doing knocked Ian's head against my bedside table, causing him to howl along with his sister.

"Oh! I forgot to congratulate you about the baby," Coach piped in. "Another little slugger, huh?"

"Thanks, Coach. I'll make those calls," I said, the phone beginning to slip from my shoulder.

"Great. And I need more yellow stars!" I heard dimly as the phone fell away. It landed squarely on the toes of Emma's left foot, intensifying her wailing.

"Mom, I can't find my backpack," Sam announced, having popped into the room. "I just remembered I have to do a project for science."

"When's it due?" I yelled.

"Ummm. Tuesday. I think."

Imagine that. He remembered with a day to spare.

◆   ◆   ◆

Ian attended his first Little League game—two of them, actually, Sam's AAA game followed by Matt dominating on the tee-ball field—when he was ten days old. Tucked in his papoose, warm and cozy against my slack belly, he snoozed away the afternoon, waking only once for me to nurse him under the shade of a generous magnolia tree that afforded a bit of privacy and offered an only partially blocked view of the tee-ball field. Baby Ian *loved* baseball—it soothed and comforted him, an otherwise fussy baby who slept little.

Due to Sam's hitting success, Coach Yellow Star called late in the season to inform me he wanted to nominate Sam for the all-star team. I began to salivate. Already fighting the melancholy that yearly accompanies the end of Little League season (complicated by post-partum depression), I dreamed of another month of baseball for Sam. There was only one problem. We had registered him for the June session of his summer camp.

"So what do you think?" I asked Sam, who responded with a look of confusion.

"Well, I have camp, don't I?"

"We might be able to work something out!" I fairly shrieked. *This was our chance at redemption!* If Sam made the team, he could make up for all those little errors and strikeouts that had blemished his all-star record in AA.

"Like what?"

"We could maybe get part of our money back?"

"You mean skip camp?"

"Uh … or switch sessions?"

"But, Mom, *everyone's* going to the three week session!"

It was true. His three best buddies would be there—his best *old* buddies, no less, those polite, innocent oldest siblings.

"Don't you *want* to be an all-star?" I blurted, letting go my self-control, giving in to the emotional blackmail I'd promised myself I wouldn't.

"Yes, I mean, no, not really …" and things went on from there. The truth was, Sam's experience with the AA all-stars had been marginal at best—marginal performance on the field and at the plate, a marginal introduction to a bunch of guys he didn't know that well. Though I would never force Sam to play all-star baseball (like some *really* nutty parents I know), worry still nagged me—would turning down a nomination reflect poorly on his chances for making the tournament team in future years?

Fate stepped in. Three days later, Sam tripped over the edge of his school track while playing soccer and broke his foot. Our resident orthopedist said no baseball, not for at least a month. So that settled it. We withdrew Sam's name from the list of all-star nominees, and Sam went to camp where he did everything from rock climbing to playing tennis to canoeing in his handy, waterproof cast. The AAA all-stars played on without him. Yet Sam's reputation remained intact—rather than turn down an invitation to play, it simply looked as if an unfortunate accident had *prevented* him from playing.

A few days after Sam's accident, we happened upon Pete Brown at the AAA championship game, the game after which the coaches would vote in the all-stars.

"What'd you do to my center-fielder?" Pete asked, eyeing Sam's cast.

"Soccer injury," I said without further explanation, leaving the impression perhaps that Sam had suffered his broken foot during a collision with a rabid midfielder in a crucial playoff game. Let him think of Sam as one those kids who plays two sports per athletic season—and plays them both well.

"Shoot." Pete looked simultaneously distressed and impressed. "We'll miss him."

"Yeah, thanks," I said. "Guess he'll go on to summer camp, after all."

As a consolation prize, my tone implied. Yet I couldn't help grinning as I carried Ian towards an empty bleacher seat. Surviving June without travel ball would be a challenge, but at least I could toss all those maternity swimsuits with the hidden tummy panels. And things for Sam looked very promising for the 2000 season, the season during which he would have his first shot at playing in Buckhead Baseball's Major Leagues.

THE SHOW

Late the following January, with Atlanta still firmly in winter's grip, Sam was drafted by Neighbor Jack's dad to play for the Major League Indians. The father of two sons, Coach Robert was a ten-year Little League veteran—and a perennial winner. When we got his call on draft night, a school night, Houston, Sam and I were so overcome with the possibilities of Sam's immediate baseball future that we launched into a giddy celebration. Not only did we anticipate many an Indians' victory, but Sam would have his buddy Jack (whom I was growing rather fond of, despite his mischievous nature) and other good friends as teammates. To boot, Robert had managed to draft a handful of former all-stars.

Euphoric, we danced and hugged and chanted a Native American war cry. Long since having snuggled into bed, Emma spilled out of her room, clapping and begging for an Indians' cheerleader dress. Matt also emerged, running headlong at Sam, leaping into his arms, straddling his body like a catcher finding the embrace of his winning pitcher. Yet by some miracle, Baby Ian snoozed peacefully throughout this revelry, no doubt with visions of his own future baseball eminence dancing in his head.

But, as it did during Sam's ill-fated Rookie season, something went tragically wrong. Come early April, the Indians were six games into the season, and our record was—I can hardly bear the memory even now—0 and 6. Zero and six, that is, meaning *no wins and six losses,* and none of them particularly close. To deepen my agony, my firstborn, my Silver Slugger, was "o-fer," as baseball lingo goes, meaning zero hits for however many at-bats he'd had. Goose egg, no hits in exactly *fourteen* at-bats, Houston reminded me.

Now that Sam was playing in The Show and since the rigors of his orthopedic practice had slowed somewhat, Houston had plunged into Sam's baseball career. Since the Indians already had a slew of dugout coaches, he volunteered to be the team statistician, a natural progression after our days with Coach Yellow Star. All Houston need do was pirate that fancy computer program. Only there was no challenge in that, sort of like asking for directions when lost. He chose instead to surf the Web himself, and having found an even more sophisticated version of Coach Yellow Star's program, began supplying Coach Robert (who before had kept up with only the basics—hits, runs, maybe RBIs and errors on a good day) with everything from TBB (total bases on balls) to slugging percentages.

"Look at this!" he called one evening after dinner.

Across the monitor screen stretched a full-color bar graph displaying each little Indian's contact percentage. That's the number of times out of total swings they actually make contact with the ball rather than whiffing, foul balls included.

"Robert's going to use this to determine his batting order."

I eyed the graph, took note that *Sam Payne's* bright orange bar was significantly shorter than, say, three-fourths of his teammates.

Super, I couldn't help but think. *Our son will bat ninth!*

As is so often the case in baseball, Sam's early season hitting slump defied all reason. In preparation for his debut in the Majors, I'd been periodically taking him for private hitting lessons. His instructor was a volunteer coach, but like many of the most devoted coaches, Coach Roger invested so much time on baseball, it put a squeeze on his work time. To compensate, he tacked on a side job—teaching hitting and pitching to Little Leaguers from all over Atlanta. Such private baseball coaches somehow manage to charge about twice what a good academic tutor makes—anywhere from $60–$100 an hour to try and correct the hitch in Junior's swing or to teach him to sling a changeup. But (as I've often rationalized) the hitting coach can be more than just a teacher. A good one is a mentor, a self-esteem builder, *a strong male authority figure* for maturing boys.

Years before, Coach Roger had finagled some space in and around an old warehouse where he set up his *office* and batting cages. One late July day the summer before his Majors' debut, Sam and I swung open the two-inch-thick metal door to this office and were greeted by a gust of hot, dusty air smelling of mildewed plastic. Bats of various lengths and weights rested in a corner near a pile of oversized mesh bags swollen with batting helmets and catcher's gear. In another corner, batting screens and infield rakes leaned against a stack of tarps. Rattling in the room's only window, an industrial-sized fan tried, and failed, to fend off the sticky heat.

Yet Coach Roger seemed immune to his prickly surroundings. Grinning, his baby blue eyes twinkling rather absurdly above his bulky and decidedly manly frame, he rose up from a chip-edged linoleum desk and extended to us his meaty right hand. His weathered skin setting off the deep silver of his bushy hair, he gave some encouraging words and described his teaching methods while Sam twirled his bat, scritching it along the concrete floor and responding in curt monosyllables. His spiel complete, Coach Roger then scooped up his metal folding chair and rearranged it a few feet in front of the room's back wall, loosely covered by a net suspended from the wall's corners.

"Let's see what you got," he began, settling his weight into the chair and pointing to a stained and ragged home plate near Sam's feet. Coach Roger leaned down to nab a few whiffle balls out of a converted paint tub and waited. Sam glanced at me. I shrugged before putting it all together just as Coach spoke again.

"Well, are you ready?"

"Oh. Yessir," Sam said. Though tormented by self-doubt, he'd played enough baseball to figure that with a bat in hand and a plate at foot, there was only one thing to do.

Still he hesitated.

"Ready?" Coach Roger asked, ball poised and clearly getting a bit impatient.

"Yessir, but I'm a lefty."

"Well, why didn't you say so, son?" He smiled broadly, revealing teeth yellowed from some form of tobacco use. "I don't bite."

Cheeks reddening, Sam quickly found his batting stance as Coach Roger shifted his chair to the other side of the plate to prepare for what's known as *soft toss*. Sitting dangerously close to where the arc of Sam's swing would pass, he tossed whiffle ball after whiffle ball into Sam's strike zone as Sam blasted each one into the net. I began slowly to back out of the room, having been given nothing resembling a *we'll see you in an hour!* or even a good-bye, yet feeling a bit the intruder.

Coach Roger waved. "We'll move outside to hit in the cage. And pitch some, too!" he called. "And I *like* his swing," he added with a thoughtful wink, as if he'd never *seen* such a swing. How it warmed this mother's heart.

◆   ◆   ◆

"Mom! Look!" Sam gushed, no trace of the teen in his little boy voice.

Having just completed lesson number two with Coach Roger, he grasped two of my fingers the way he used to as a toddler and guided me across the office. Tacked randomly across the wall was a regular photo gallery of Mark McGwire wannabes, many of them Sam's former all-star teammates, some of them his tournament foes from NFYO, and all apparently devoted protégés of the famous Coach Roger. One or two older boys grinned and slouched, their bats tipped with confidence over their shoulders like a cast-off raincoat. Others, mostly younger, were singled out as happy recipients of a variety of hitting honors.

"No, look at *this*, Mom," Sam said, pointing at a can of Dr. Pepper with black markings scrawled across it.

"Uhhhh, that's great, honey. What is it?"

"I'm in the Dr. Pepper Club. Already! Coach says it takes most guys three or four visits *at least* to hit the can."

Hit the can?

"See, he has this can, well not this one but one just like it, way up in the net, the cage net, it's sort of stuck in there, then he pitches to you, like, inside, outside, down the middle, then if you can hit the can, you're in the club. And I did it!"

"Great!" I squeezed his shoulders, bony and jittery with the thrill of victory.

"Yessir, he was one of the quickest to get in the club," said Coach Roger, coming up behind us, in search of his paycheck, no doubt. Beaming at him, Sam wriggled out of my arms. Coach whacked him on the back so hard he jolted forwards.

"'Cept for maybe ol' Slugger there. He hit the can first try." Coach Roger's fleshy forefinger smudged a photo of one of Sam's tee-ball teammates, none other than Gus, the Buckhead underachiever-turned-NFYO superstar. Sure enough, SLUGGER was written under his photo.

"And Jack, of course." Roger pointed out the familiar impish face of Neighbor Jack. "Nothin' much to him, but he can sure slam the ball."

Jack's nickname read simply, BABE.

Sam's smile began to fade as Roger thrust a pin through an underdeveloped Polaroid then mounted it directly under Neighbor Jack's devilish grin. Slowly, Sam's sheepish smile emerged from the celluloid. The bat over his shoulder appeared too large, a burden. In uneven cursive, Coach Roger jotted a nickname—CHAMP. Perfect, as if Sam were a feisty English setter who'd just won Best in Show.

"Yeah, before you know it, Champ here'll have his name up *there*," he said, pointing to a high corner of his display. "We'll start timing your swing next lesson."

And there it was: The true elite, a list of boys' names, each with a number and MPH scribbled after it, sort of like a NASCAR log book.

I laughed, feigning complicity, and patted Sam on the back to urge him towards the exit.

"What exactly does he time?" I asked gingerly as we approached the car.

"Bat speed, *Mom*," Sam spat, as if explaining the obvious to an imbecile. "That's how fast those guys can swing the bat. Mine's not good enough even to go at the *bottom* of the list."

He chucked his bat bag into the back of our van and slammed the tailgate.

"How do you know?" I asked. "I thought he said he'd time you *next* lesson."

"I just know," Sam mumbled, staring away, retreating to his prepubescent world.

Sam continued his hitting lessons well into that first Majors' season, but come late April, with his orange bar limping towards .150 on the graph (he'd had maybe three hits, one of them a bunt single), I decided to lay off. At $65 a pop, ol' Roger wasn't exactly earning his keep, and Sam's surliness seemed to expand in an inverse relationship to the dwindling of his CRSP. Though I didn't realize it at the time, he was in the throes of what Little League veterans would call a *typical eleven-year-old season*. Because eleven- and twelve-year-olds play together in the Majors, Sam, scrawny Sam, was suddenly pitting his skills with the bat against towering twelve-year-olds, some of whom God had graced with that elusive physical phenomenon envied by many a Little League father—*early onset puberty*. At four foot ten, Sam would sometimes step up to bat against five-foot-seven-inches worth of grit and whiskers on the mound. Could you blame him for backing away from the plate when he witnessed the baseball hurtling towards him from the beefy arms of those adolescent monsters?

As often happens, one manager in particular during this millennium season had connived to field an entire team full of such robust genetic mutations. Whereas our Coach Robert had lost his most promising twelve-year-old player to a more *competitive program* during the Indians' off-season, Coach Gip Johnston of the Yankees had achieved managerial nirvana. The 2000 Yankees' roster included not only a regiment of twelve-year-olds who could bench press the equivalent of a Hummer limo, but also a couple of first years with early birthdays whose biceps were responding to early infusions of testosterone. By the time of our first meeting with them in mid-April, the Yankees' win-loss record was a mirror image of the Indians' game tally at 2-7. The boys in pinstripes were 7-2 and tied for first place.

Clearly, our work was cut out for us. I'd like to be able to say Coach Robert followed his best instincts and fielded for this game his strongest defense backed by our ace on the mound. Instead, he approached the game like Chuck Tanner after a lobotomy. With none but the most noble intentions, he decided to mix things up in the infield and tamper with the batting order. Most painful of all, he called on Sam to serve as our starting pitcher.

Having hurled a few winning games during his Majors' fall ball season (a kinder, gentler season of baseball), Sam (and I) did have hopes of reviving his pitching career, cowering and dormant though it had become during his tour with Coach Yellow Star. Coach Robert had complied by promising to give Sam some innings on the mound. However, the Indians already had a strong twelve-year-old pitcher, plus Robert's son, Jack, whose *pre*-Majors ERA had been around 0.47. Then there was Jack's best friend's best friend, who also pitched and whose father was the Indians' assistant coach. Seeing as how, in comparison with these starters, Sam was underdeveloped, not to mention under-confident due to his anemic orange bar, we were halfway through the season, and he'd been called on to pitch for exactly one inning, in relief, with mixed results (walked two and gave up three hits before tallying a single out). Why not start him against the top team in the league?

The Indians were the visiting team that balmy April Saturday. During our first at-bat, two Indians actually reached base but only thanks to bases on balls resulting from the Yankees' pitcher Stu experiencing early game jitters. No one but our lone twelve-year-old star had even dared to swing at Stu's terrifying split-finger fastball.

After tallying the last out of the inning, swinging and missing and stranding those two runners, Sam climbed to the crest of the mound and drew in a deep, yoga-like breath before launching into his warm-up pitches. The first three Yankee batters, tall, lean twelve-year-olds, stepped out of their dugout wearing batting helmets stamped with the *New York* Yankees' latest monogram. One leaning against his bat, another slouching with hands on hips, the three eyed Sam while laughing easily together, blowing bubbles created from wads of Big League Chew surely provided by their (type A) team mom. At a subtle hand gesture from Coach Gip, however, they spread apart behind the on-deck circle and lifted bats to shoulders nearly in unison, hawkeyed on Sam's motion. As Sam took his final pitches, pitches that bobbled and jumped around the strike zone, sending his catcher into exaggerated body contortions in the effort to control them, these future Mickey Mantles crouched into perfect stances. As each pitch sailed in, they swung their bats violently across imaginary home plates.

"Balls in!" called the umpire. Recognizing this voice, I pried my eyes away from the mound to confirm my worst fear. *It was the Nazi.* Tall and slickly muscular himself, he oversaw Sam's warm-up with arms folded brusquely across his chest protector. His ump's mask dangling from the long, sinewy fingers of his left hand, he rocked on his heels like a regular General Patton. His face, handsome in a sharp, severe way, spread into a sinister grin when Sam's final pitch bounced a foot in front of home plate then careened to the backstop. The catcher scrambled to fetch the ball, which ricocheted, pinball-style, and bounced to within inches of the man in blue himself. Sly eyes still fixed on Sam, the Nazi lifted his left foot and popped his ankle, creating a sort of human lever arm to propel the ball back towards the plate.

This was an umpire of some repute around Buckhead Baseball, notorious among mothers in particular for his tight strike zone and religious dedication to the bylaws handed down by Little League, Inc.'s national board of directors. One hand shading my eyes, I watched as he pulled a comb out of the pocket of his neatly pressed military-gray slacks. After smoothing back his hair, he pulled on his mask and replaced the comb. Protruding from the slacks' back pocket was the upper corner of a dog-eared copy of the Little League rule book.

"Coming down!" cried our catcher. I rubbed my temples, hoping to quell the early stages of a headache and to occupy my fingers lest they slip into their old habit of compulsive pill rolling. It wasn't that I or any other mother favored breaking the rules—rules, a consistent strike zone, a steady eye, these are the framework on which any good umpire is built—but being mothers, most of us had learned that where little boys and sports were concerned, at times rules must be bent to protect delicate egos. The Nazi *liked* mothers (perhaps a hair more than he did boys). He loved nothing more, in fact, than to stand near the first base bleachers between innings and chitchat, infusing his dialogue with numerous colorful references to his intricate knowledge of the game of baseball. Maybe it was due to the munificent size of his own ego, maybe to some twisted version of tough love, but the Nazi had not a dot of empathy for our fragile sons.

"Play ball!" he called gruffly.

The crowd quieted. Sam straightened up as tall as his preteen muscles would stretch and threw one fastball strike, followed by one of the juiciest, most unhittable curves a lefty could throw. As it angled into the catcher's mitt, poised on the outside corner of the plate, I held my breath and waited for the call. The batter, who hadn't so much as offered at the pitch, gazed stolidly at the plate. Being a highly disciplined Yankee, Coach Gip's lead-off man, no less, he had surely been subjected not only to daily hand-eye drills to improve his patience as a hitter, but also to long seminars on the importance of bluffing as a tool in influencing the umpire.

But it had been a very good pitch, even by professional standards, a pitch Tom Glavine might have thrown early in a game to impress the umpire and establish a generous strike zone. The Nazi hesitated, leaning ever so slightly towards the perfect *V* of the catcher's elbow. He had framed Sam's pitch so beautifully, this diminutive Indians' catcher, held ball in mitt with such hope and loyalty it nearly brought me to tears. I waited, willing the Nazi's fist off of his knee and into that wonderful hand jerk that would accompany the *Aaargh* of a called strike. Instead he relaxed, stood, and stepped back on one foot, letting his arms fall slack, his right hand flicking weakly to the right, sending down the verdict that the pitch had been a touch outside.

Ball one, followed sadly by balls two through four. I stood to vacate my seat and venture up the third-base line where I couldn't see Sam's face. A few years later, after I watched a strong left-handed pitcher on Sam's high school team walk in three runs, I would finally admit that control issues are simply the hallmark of a young lefty. At the time, of course, I chalked up Sam's inability to find the strike zone to my own shortcomings as a mother. After the Yankees number-two hitter ripped a double, Sam went on and walked two more batters. I rued the day I ever suggested to Coach Robert that he pitch.

The bases were now full of Yanks, and we trailed by a run. After tossing yet another ball, Sam was met at the foul line by the Indians' pitching coach, who rocked in towards Sam's face, gripping his shoulders, calming his nerves. Encouraged, Sam induced the next Yankee to hit a weak pop-up to short. Although the pond was still full of ducks, he'd forced that crucial first out. His next pitch boded well, too. The batter, an oversized eleven-year-old named Jeff, swung and missed at Sam's fastball.

"Don't give me that!" said Gip, coaching third. "You're a *Yankee*. Now swing like one!"

Undaunted, Sam served up another nasty curve, one that painted, this time, the inside corner.

Again, we moms held our breath.

Again, the Nazi, our judge and executioner, hesitated, then ruled the pitch a ball.

"See!" Gip cried, heatedly clapping. "This guy can't find the plate—he's got *nothing*! If it's close, *crush it*!"

My jaw clenched—*Had he really said that? Had anyone else heard it?*

I looked at Sam, who had most certainly heard. Shoulders slouched, arms dangling limp by his sides, for a brief moment, he turned towards Gip and stared, his eyes bright with pain and laced with a look of confused panic. I thought of Isaac, standing with Abraham before the sacrificial altar, wondering how an adult he trusted could betray him so completely.

"Base hit. *Now!*" Gip continued, and in his defense, he was blind to the hurt I read in Sam's face. (At the time, Gip had no sons of playing age.) Over the next two years, we, Sam included, would come to know Gip well, to love him as a manager, a loyal friend, and to understand that like many of the best Little League coaches, he sometimes erred on the side of winning, perhaps over encouraged his own boys, particularly when they were playing their best ball. Gip's players usually responded well to his methods; their parents swore by the dedication and discipline he demanded from them. But on this day, with a little help from the Nazi, he was threatening to crush the already shaky confidence of a certain Indian on the mound.

"Come on, Sam!" called Coach Robert from the dugout, doing his best to counter the negative vibes. "You got a whole infield behind you. Use it!"

I glanced at Sam. Resolute, he shrugged his shoulders again, this time shaking off the blanket of bad karma that had enfolded him since the Nazi's first stringent call.

"Just throw strikes, Sam!" I called, resisting the urge to follow this up with a little payback, something to the effect of, *This guy couldn't hit the side of a barn!*

Sam did throw another strike, a fastball beauty that clipped the edge of the strike zone. Jeff swung, to no avail.

Next, a curve, one too close to take. Jeff fouled it off but hard, just outside the third-base line. Sam, jumpy, then shook off the curve sign from his catcher and went with yet another fastball. This time, Gip's endless drills paid off. Jeff went with the pitch and drove it to deep center, scoring two more runs.

"Attaboy, Jeff!" Gip screamed through cupped hands to his runner on second. "Keep it up, Yankees!"

Keep it up they did. An error on our second baseman's part led to another run. Flustered, Sam then threw a wild pitch, allowing Jeff to score.

It was 5-0, Yankees, with one out and a man on second. Feeling a touch nauseated, I slid behind the rough chain-link fence and sat on the grass, hardly noticing how damp it was. Sam looked to his dugout, fearful yet at the same time perhaps hopeful that his time on the mound might be up. I knew what was running through the mind of all our coaches, all the parents, for that matter. Do you pull Sam this early to preserve a chance at a comeback? Or do you show confidence in him, at least give him a chance to record another out?

Robert went with the second plan, and the Indians and their coaches showered Sam with encouraging words. "You can do it, Lassie!" I heard from sweet little old Jack, using Sam's nickname as he walked jauntily towards a strip of grass near the outfield foul line that served as a bull pen. I've never been so happy to see a boy warming up to pitch—no matter what came of Sam's outing, Jack, the unflappable Jack, would be able to come in and patch things up.

Newly buoyed, Sam stared down the Yankees' next hitter with eagle-like precision and split the plate with a called strike, then induced a foul ball before turning once again to his lovely curve. It was a familiar scenario—with the count 0 and 2, the batter was in a deep hole. *Everyone* knew the next pitch would be something off-speed.

"Watch for the curve!" called Gip, finally showing Sam a glimmer of respect. The pitch did not disappoint—it started two feet above the batter's head but dropped across the right edge of the strike zone and into the carefully placed catcher's mitt, right where he'd wanted it.

"That's it, buddy!" I called, but too soon. Yet again, the Nazi judged the pitch outside.

"Aaawww, come on, Blue!" spat at least three Indians' dads, no longer able to control their tongues. "Put your glasses on!" one of them continued. *And who could blame him?* This was Little League, we were down by five in the first. It was time to cut Sam and the Indians a little slack, move the game along. Even a few Yankees' moms were mumbling about this call.

Perhaps it was due to poor parental example, perhaps to years of pent-up frustration over control issues, but Sam at that point committed one of Little League's mortal sins: after receiving the throw from his catcher, he paused, waiting for the Nazi to face the mound again. Certain he had his attention, Sam then lifted shoulders to earlobes, thrust up his lower arms like he was getting set to juggle, and gave the Nazi what could only be called the evil eye. Despite his self-absorption, he caught Sam's drift. Heck, I think five-year-old Emma caught it as she ran up from the playground to ask for concession-stand money.

What the hell more can I do? Sam's gesture implied, and although he had every right to feel this way, he was not allowed to show it. A *good* umpire would have called time, perhaps met with Sam and his catcher on the mound to explain his call and review the parameters of his strike zone. A *good* umpire might have reprimanded Sam, given him fair warning of disciplinary measures for challenging a call. A *good* umpire would have approached the situation like an adult who'd been charged with training young athletes in the game's rules as well as its etiquette. I've seen many good umpires treat anxious players in this way.

Not this umpire. He stood stock still, glaring, for several seconds, until Sam, eyes filling, was forced to look away. Sam wiped his eyes on his sleeve as the Nazi waved viciously for him to bring on the next pitch. His beady eyes still fixed on Sam, his mouth pinched and hard, his broad back stiff and unyielding, he leaned in over the catcher yet again.

It may be unnecessary to say that things went from bad to worse. The strike zone shrank from small to infinitesimal. Sam tossed a few wild pitches, and our poor catcher, already filthy and exhausted in this, still the first inning, floundered. Gip, not one to miss an opportunity, encouraged his boys to steal on any ball that got away. A few more hits, couple walks later, we were down 12-0. I suppressed my own tears as Sam continued to wipe at his eyes, this time with a grimy palm, streaking his tender cheeks with pale orange. Having no other choice, Robert called Jack in from the bull pen. His tall, thin body hunched with regret and concern, Robert patted Sam on the rear as he handed over the ball. At that point, I went ahead and cried.

Jack managed to get out of the inning, but not before a few Yankees hit doubles, a couple more walked, and a few stole home. Come the top of the second, the score was Yankees 18, Indians 0. We did score a couple of runs later in the game, just after Sam struck out again with men in scoring position. Sam's batting average dropped only a couple of points, but his ERA ticked in at a crisp 329.0. And guess what? It hovered there well into his *next* season with the Indians. Although I tried to encourage him, suggested that perhaps a few private *pitching* lessons might be just the thing, I began to detect a certain destructive pattern in his behavior whenever I mentioned pitching. This behavior ranged from surly glances to fists thrust perilously close to windows and Sheetrock walls. Hoping to preserve his hands for outfield catches, not to mention pass receptions during the coming football season, I placed a temporary moratorium on counseling Sam about his sports' career.

His bat, however, always the more dependable aspect of his game, began to heat up late in that eleven-year-old season. Despite his pitching woes, Sam dug in, overcame his fear of being beaned, and learned to hit the curve. At first, everything he hit hard went right at an opposing defender for an out. But gradually, some bloop hits, then some line drives, began to fall in. One afternoon, I happened to be watching from the same spot along the outfield fence where I'd witnessed the Yankees' debacle. As usual, gathered near me was a group of dads and coaches from other teams.

Sam drilled a rope nearly to the fence and was standing on third by the time the ball made it back to the infield.

"Who woke up Sam?" a familiar voice asked.

"Yeah. Been punishing the ball," our opposing pitcher's father answered glumly to none other than Pete Brown, coach of the Buckhead Tournament Team.

When Pete looked past his depressed comrade to give me a smile and a wink, the knot I'd felt in my belly since that first Yankees' game began to loosen, ever so slightly. Although the Indians' season finished unremarkably, and Sam was not nominated for all-stars, there was always next year.

That is, for one last, splendid time, there was next year.

A Little Extra BP

Come the first of July, we packed the older boys off to camp in the mountains of North Carolina. Though it was Matt's first year, Sam was by this time a veteran camper. For such a highly competitive kid, he ironically adored the entire summer camp experience and would talk for months about the rock climbing and mountain biking in his near future. He even enjoyed twisting the occasional lanyard out of twine, and all under the tutelage of well-balanced young men and women who focused on developing camper self-esteem through harmonizing with one's natural environment. For Sam, these weeks away offered the perfect counterbalance to the stress of the high-intensity play characteristic of the Majors.

With the boys out of the house and Emma in day camp, I, however, ended up with too much time on my hands, perhaps too many long, buggy, dog day afternoons to endure while Ian bubbled around in the comfort of his plastic pool. No surprise that I fell off the redemptive wagon and allowed my idle, errant brain to circle back to the mediocrity of Sam's recent season. I ran through, incessantly, the many ways in which he'd come up short, from strikeout to pop-up to the searing image of his tear-laced shrug at the Nazi after the heartbreak of Gip's insults. I fretted, sensing also as I approached my fortieth birthday, that time and my boys' golden years were spinning away.

One quiet sweltering afternoon as Ian napped, I wandered out to the mailbox and returned sweating and heavily laden with junk mail. As I tossed pizza circulars and credit card promotions into the trash, a shiny flyer printed in red, black and blue caught my eye—DOUBLE YOUR SLUGGER'S BATTING AVERAGE IN TWO SHORT WEEKS! one headline read. And more—A 20 PERCENT INCREASE IN POWER—GUARANTEED!

I yanked the flyer out of the slush pile, cranked up the AC, and sank into a mound of cool pillows on the couch. The flyer, sent from a baseball supply company called *Future All-Stars,* was addressed not to RESIDENT but more specifically to MARTHA AND HOUSTON PAYNE, a fact that somehow validated the mailing for me—*Did perhaps only former tournament team players, boys with recognized potential, receive such?* In retrospect, I have no doubt that the parent of every Little Leaguer in the combined fifty states received this flyer, yet my baseball-deprived mind chose to grasp at every tendril of hope.

I turned the pages slowly, drooling over photos of young players swinging and hitting in the comfort of their own backyards. A two-page spread featured boys and girls pitching off of portable mounds into a variety of nets and backstops while their younger siblings played on swing sets or tousled with puppies. Another presented batting gloves and catcher's equipment in the brightest of colors. A few pages in, I got to the really good stuff—pitching machines and do-it-yourself batting cages. As I reviewed the various nets and frames, I revisited a passing thought I'd had after picking Sam up from a teammate's house a few weeks earlier. The teammate, one of four children himself, had just been elected an all-star and he owned, Sam said, in the expansive backyard of his expansive home, a *batting cage*. I'd yearned at the time to question Sam about this, to explore the potential boost owning such a cage might give my boys, but Ian was screaming for a bottle of juice, and Emma's hair was tangled in her new bracelet, and, well, the moment had passed.

Yet here was proof—batting cages were not exclusive to youth baseball parks and the offices of hitting instructors like Coach Roger. Regular people owned them! Well, maybe not *regular* but everyday people concerned with furthering their children's Little League careers. And you could build one yourself—*in six easy steps*!

When Houston later dragged home from the hospital, I couldn't help but share my happy news.

"Where would it go?" he asked.

Details!

"Straight across the backyard. Way in the back."

"Oh, the back. It's not level."

"Level, schmevel. Can't we flatten it out or something?"

"Maybe, but it would have to be cleared, too."

"Well, I figured that."

"And what about the pitching machine?"

"They have those, too!"

I thrust the flyer under his nose, its bodacious promises front and center.

He scanned the full-color photos, one eyebrow twitching with interest. I just knew he was visualizing as I had been—*because of our cage, Sam slugs his way onto the All-Star Team and beyond, onto his high school varsity where he's immediately the top hitter on the team and thus has time to bloom as a pitcher, gaining the size and discipline required to develop his left-*

handed knuckleball (which, of course, he has practiced in our cage that easily converts into a pitching tunnel). Then before you can say Gold Glove, he's making diving catches in center at Turner Field, where the 2012 Braves (thanks to Sam and our cage) are just a few weeks shy of clinching the division title.

Houston flipped through the flyer, barely pausing to admire the glossies of new-fangled gear I hoped to purchase for Matt, our budding catcher, then turned to the back page, where in heartless black ink loomed the price list.

"I don't know," he said, rubbing two fingers at his temple. "This doesn't even include the price of *building* the cage."

"But it's Sam's last year!" I pressed, hesitating to add, *Remember his sickly orange bar?*

Still, the moment was wrong. I got a *Let's think about it,* a comment that left me feeling hangdog as a child denied a new toy. Things had been slow at work, and, oh yeah, we'd already earmarked several thousand dollars as yet to be earned for the little business of tacking a family room on to our house. So I tucked the flyer into the back of my overstuffed file labeled BOYS' SPORTS and determined to find another way to further my cause.

◆   ◆   ◆

The task of ripping off our old deck began around the time Sam and Matt started back to school. In fact, the fall of 2000 brought Emma's initiation into *real* school as well, and I found myself at home with a couple of builders and only one child for six hours a day. The demolition phase proved a godsend as Ian at a year and a half was more distracted by watching these burly men slashing away with their axes and sledge hammers than he was by *Sesame Street.* Stage two was a delight for all: the laying of the foundation. Our contractor didn't do this sort of work himself (way too messy) but instead brought in a team of guys whose job it was to dig and reconfigure and level the Georgia red clay of our backyard before laying a maze of wooden planks to serve as molds for the concrete.

This small-to-medium sized project required a throng of workers. A dapper Venezuelan (we'll call him Luis) supervised the group. Luis wore polo shirts and khakis, and from the looks of him, never personally touched concrete or fill dirt, but he could converse in perfect English with me while simultaneously firing orders in staccato Spanish to his crew of workers, most of whom we think were legal immigrants. No matter, these men were efficient, elaborate in their concentration. One *Vámanos!* from Luis, and they joyously whipped into action—straightening boards and eyeing leveling string and mitering corners.

One afternoon after school, the five of us sat squinting through the sheet of plastic that had once been the picture window overlooking our deck. Far below, a few of Luis's men, armed with squared-off shovels, zig-zagged through the clay swift as a pair of moles.

"How do they do it so *fast?*" Matt asked, eyes huge with wonder.

"They're good at it," I answered, tightening my vice grip on Ian who, determined that he should burst through and offer his excavating skills, whined incessantly. "Dig! Dig!" he squealed.

"Don't they get tired?" Matt continued.

"Sure, but it's their job."

"*Yeah*, Matt, not everybody gets to *pick* what they want to do like Dad," Sam railed from his sixth-grade soapbox.

"Not everybody *wants* to do work like Dad's," I added in an effort to make a sociopolitical lesson of the moment.

"Yeah, *Sam*," Matt snarled.

At dinner that evening, I mustered the courage to reintroduce the touchy subject of the batting cage. When Houston continued to balk at the price tag, I offered a suggestion.

"Maybe we could build it ourselves."

"Right, Mom," Sam pounced. "Like *you're* gonna be out there with a shovel."

Remembering, no doubt, my lack of skill at building block towers or even arranging dollhouse furniture, Emma said with a sweet smile, "Mama, you don't build very good."

But my remark achieved its intent. Everyone loosened up on the subject, and soon ideas for construction of the anticipated cage were zipping like fireworks above our chicken and peas.

"I get to dig with the *big* shovel," said Matt.

"Me, too!" cried Emma.

"No way!" answered Sam. "I'm the oldest!"

"But I called it!"

"Let me have it, and you can hang the net with Dad," Sam coerced.

"Me, too!" cried Emma.

Though Ian fairly shrieked throughout this chatter, his gibberish garnered so little attention that he finally flung a spoonful of mashed potatoes against Matt's cheek, an action that might have ended in disaster on any other night but which, on this occasion, simply contributed to our domestic exuberance. Houston, however, only smiled and politely commended the children for their ideas. He—the one who in fact loved good old manual labor and was a perfectly capable handy man—had not added a single idea of his own. We had yet to sway him, and without his enthusiasm and approval, we were nothing. The kids must have sensed his resistance, too. Shortly after Ian plastered Matt with potato mush, their laughter dwindled, and we were enfolded in silence again, Sam twirling a fork through his leftover potatoes, and Emma staring into a hill of cold peas.

"Dig! Dig!" continued Ian, however, and not to be denied, Matt wiped his cheek, stared thoughtfully through our plastic barrier at the maze of wood planks beyond, and theorized, "Dad, why don't we just get a bunch of Mexicans to build it?"

Wrenching his neck, Houston peered out over the pit as if he expected an army of workers to be there still, dripping the blood and sweat of their impoverished ancestors into the very heart of our home, and all thanks to our evil capitalist ways. There was no one there, of course, but each of us stared a moment across the pit, dim and shadowy in the dusk, and on to the back of the property, where I at least could easily envision Luis's quiet, hard-working men toiling away to flatten our yard, tipsy as the Tower of Pisa, just so our boys might enjoy a bit of success on the Little League field.

After what seemed an eternity of silence, Emma asked coyly, "Daddy, what's a Mexican?" just as Ian swiped his entire plate of food onto the floor.

We cleaned up in a flurry, Matt's suggestion hovering over us in the humid September night.

"That Matt!" I finally exclaimed with perhaps a bit much enthusiasm. "Out of the mouths of babes!"

"Yeah, well," Houston said as he rinsed a pot, "guess he has a point."

"Yes?" I asked, heart clanging against my ribs.

"We could find some guys to do the job, I'm sure, but do we want the kids thinking you just go hire a bunch of cheap labor every time you need something done?"

We'd hit a nerve, I knew it—good ol' Puritan work ethic.

"No, but you're so busy."

"I'll check out how much it costs to rent a Bobcat. Maybe we can get the clearing and leveling done in a weekend."

He was in!

Construction of the Payne Batting Cage began soon after. Houston dug and uprooted bushes and dragged limbs and leaves for hours at a time. The boys pitched in best they could and Emma wandered out now and again, a plastic beach shovel in hand. The real work began after a huge truck from our local Home Depot delivered "Biff" the Bobcat one Friday afternoon, an event that in itself created a frenzy of excitement. The three older children descended on the little tractor like buzzards on roadkill, yanking the steering wheel, pulling knobs, poking greasy engine parts.

"Mom, can I drive it?" hollered Sam before Mr. Home Depot could even clear his running board.

"Of course not," I said, an image of my firstborn plowing over his siblings rising in my mind. "Where are the keys?"

"Got 'em!" said Sam, a sly grin on his face and a set of keys dangling from his pinky finger. "Please, Mom? Just on the driveway?"

"*No, Sam,*" I said firmly. "Give me the keys."

He grimaced, stopping just shy of sticking out his tongue, then tossed me the keys with a touch too much vigor and sulked off, leaving Matt and Emma to squabble over who would get the first ride later with Dad.

The northeastern fringe of a hurricane swept through Atlanta that night and into Saturday morning. Through our plastic screen, we watched torrents of mud wash into the trenches of our would-be foundation. The nascent pit of our future cage suffered as well. Foul pools rose up under branches and mounds of leaves which we had thought were stowed securely at the low end of the yard. These began to float back over the clean edges that just hours earlier had marked the site where our precious net would hang. The edges of the pit themselves began to ooze inward until, alas, what on Friday had allowed our imaginations to conjure a batting tunnel Bobby Cox might himself freely boast over was now a muddy bog.

When a few rays of sun broke through the engorged gray skies on Saturday afternoon, Houston tentatively maneuvered Biff around the slushy perimeter of Luis's workspace, through what remained of our soggy grass (leaving behind a formidable set of tread marks), and up to within a foot of the shifting earth of the cage pit. Finally, on Sunday afternoon, he was able to trim away mud and debris from the pit's edges. On Monday, we called to extend Biffy's rental, and I went on with my week, that evening leaving Sam home alone to complete a homework assignment while I drove Matt's hockey car pool. With our last player safely delivered to his cold dinner, Matt, Emma, Ian and I opened the van windows, clicked off the radio, and breezed through the neighborhood, rejoicing that autumn seemed finally to have reached the Deep South. As we approached our house, the guttural cries of a tractor motor hailed our arrival.

"Daddy's home!" Emma shrieked, spotting Houston's car and unbuckling her seat belt. Ian launched into a furious effort to break free of the straps of his car seat.

"Wait!" I cried, anxious lest she tear directly into Biff's path. But I cried in vain. She and Matt raced to the back of the house. I snatched Ian to my hip and followed their lead, absorbing mud through the gaps in my sandals yet excited in spite of myself to see what surprise progress Houston had made. The motor revved yet again just as I caught sight of Matt and Emma, standing hand in hand in wonder.

"When do I get a turn?" yelled Matt.

I hurried on only to see what I'd dreaded most: Sam in the driver's seat, grinning and waving with one hand while he drove Biff with the other like he was Dale Jr. himself. Houston sat by his side, working the lever of the claw-toothed shovel and looking not particularly worried as the Bobcat bumped and swayed and finally slogged to a halt in the face of an especially deep drift of mud.

Matt ran towards Biff, leaving Emma, too afraid to run herself yet wanting in on this amusement, staring languidly after him.

"Hold on, Matt!" called Houston as Sam pulled his body up out of the driver's seat and suspended himself momentarily in Biff's window. "Let me get it unstuck first!"

So it was true. He was planning on letting both boys drive the Bobcat through mud thick and gooey as the Mississippi Delta. Sam clambered over into the passenger seat, relenting to Houston's suggestions that maybe he should be the one to unstick Biff and thus pave the way for this family fun to continue. I trudged up to steady Matt on the sidelines, my right arm screaming with the pain of holding Ian as he repeatedly tried to launch his body into the mud by executing backbends over my elbow.

Houston turned the key and Biff complied, though I could hear a tinny little whine in his rumble I hadn't detected before.

"Hi, Mom!" called Sam, grinning still, and Houston waved and smiled himself. He pressed Biff's gas pedal, desperate for added power, and even Emma winced to hear the Bobcat struggle against the slippery earth. Yet the treads caught and Biff gunned backwards, throwing Sam and Houston into an immediate reverse whiplash. We all, Ian included, as I recall, let out the breath we hadn't even known we were holding.

"Be right over, Matt!" Houston called as he sped towards the back end of the pit, the *steep* end. Briefly, I wondered why he would exit the mud at that precipitous angle, yet I worried little, so confident was I in Houston's ability to maneuver Biff. His judgment with reference to letting the kids drive I worried about, his driving *skills*, I didn't. But alas, he was asking a bit much of the feisty bobcat. Biff capsized, tipped clear over, but S-L-O-W-L-Y, listing left and sinking as if trapped in quicksand. Once all motion stopped, Houston lay ear-first in a bed of mud with Sam sprawled across his lap.

For the next couple of days (during which an insidious light rain continued to fall), neither father nor sons could bring himself to go anywhere near Biff, who lay forlornly in the mud at a three-quarter slant, costing us a hefty daily babysitting fee, for what seemed weeks. I hesitated to mention to Houston (so long-faced was he after failing in his mission) that if we couldn't afford the cage before, we'd never pay for it if we didn't finish up with the leveling and get Biff back to the barn.

By Friday morning, however, I was figuring enough was enough. While I cleaned up the breakfast mess, I heard a rustle against our plastic shield. Lost in thought, I'd all but forgotten about our contractor's first mate who was there to frame up a wall.

"'Scuse me, ma'am?"

"Yes, come on in, Mike."

"You want me to work on that Bobcat?" he asked, careful not to insinuate that there was anything particularly unusual about its position relative to the earth. "I used to drive them. In my other job."

"Sure. Do you think you can budge it?"

"I can sure try," he said with a smile, and with that, it was done. I handed over the keys, and with no further insult to Houston's pride, Biff was righted.

In fact, by sundown, the pit was mostly level. At no extra charge.

◆   ◆   ◆

A week or so before Christmas (well before the January VISA statement arrived), I revisited my file folder and pulled out that old July issue flyer from the Future All-Stars company. Maybe I dreamed it, but it somehow still smelled like new ink, its glossy paper freshly printed. I reviewed again its seductive photo essay then pressed a Post-It note at the top corner. *Thought it might be a good time to order some supplies,* I wrote. *Opening Day is less than three months away! Thanks!* I then shoved a stack of bills to the side of Houston's desk and set the flyer in their place. Soon we ordered a cage net, supplies for a wooden frame, and a pitching machine—one that could mimic the curve and be set to pitch at several different speeds.

On a certain Sunday evening in late February, Atlanta enjoyed one of those warm, dewy early spring days that gives her inhabitants the strength to endure the long, humid summer ahead. Wearing a cotton sweater and jeans, I sat breathing in the sweet smell of spring and reading in a lawn chair on our newly reconfigured deck as Ian and Emma played on the swing set below me. Out back, Sam and Matt were handing up the final sections of net for Houston to secure to the cage posts. The sun shone brightly through the crisp green branches of a Bradford pear covered in happy buds. A light breeze shifted through tall daffodil shoots, the bulbs of which had somehow dodged the teeth of Biff's shovel. Matt ran by me, headed for the garage.

"Mom, when's dinner?" Emma called, racing up the deck stairs. Covered in dirt and shoots of immature grass, Ian toddled up behind her, just as I heard the unmistakable clink of a metal bat being dragged across our driveway.

"Soon, honey," I said, resisting the tug of duty a while longer.

"It's done, Mom!" cried Matt racing past, and sure enough, moments later, Sam stood in to hit, the angles of his body surely sharper, his legs surely lankier than just the day before. When Houston unleashed a pitch, he swung for the fences, sent the ball deep into the mesh behind his father's head. The cables held. The ball fell dead on the gravel, and our cage had been christened, the cage that might have been six months in the making, but that had been made by hand, the old-fashioned way. Although its existence was rooted in a mother's fanaticism, its creation had been a family affair, and the satisfaction I saw on Sam's face as he took his first swings seemed deeper than that borne of simply putting bat on ball.

And Matt was up next.

DUCKS ON THE POND

Perhaps thanks to the convenience of our home cage Sam approached his twelve-year-old baseball season, his final season of Little League, with more anticipation than anxiety. It helped, too, that as a sixth grader, he'd made the jump to junior high and was one of the big kids now, the bottom of the food chain but nevertheless walking the same halls, eating the same lunches, as boys with prom dates and college placement on their minds rather than trading cards and Gameboys. It's a sad moment for a boy-mother, that day when her son exchanges his camouflage tee and bed-rumpled hair for collared shirts and a pocket comb, but it's inevitable.

And it's these boys, these high-minded sixth graders, who make the Majors such a unique and irresistible place. After long years of watching swaggering twelve-year-olds play high-intensity ball, *real* baseball, it's finally their turn. This progression is only made sweeter by the dubious and difficult nature of the first Majors season, which can be a trial for even the best players. My Sam and his brother Matt had a combined grand total of thirteen hits when they were eleven. That's thirteen hits in, oh, 220 innings?

Ouch.

Yet Sam, long since a Little League grad, seems to have little memory of his wimpy eleven-year-old performance at the plate. And why should he? Why should any player who has survived such ignominy and gone on to experience the grandeur of being a senior Little Leaguer fret over a bulging ERA or a mere five months of poor hitting? Are they even the same people from one year to the next?

Many parents have wondered just this as they sit on the identical stretch of bleacher they laid claim to the year before. The boy who steps up to the plate on Opening Day of his twelve-year-old season certainly resembles their son, but in nine cases out of ten, most everything about him has altered somehow. His arms and legs are longer, his hair perhaps curlier or thicker and almost certainly darker, the nose and jawbone and brow line perhaps more pronounced and angular, and of course, the face whose soft, gentle features just a year earlier betrayed a look of dread and terror now displays a cocky smile, even a scowl from time to time, one intended to *induce* dread in the eleven-year-olds out in the field. Although precious few players at twelve sport facial hair and have to deal with the joys of acne and the voice change, a visible transformation often does occur between seasons. This transformation is what Majors' coaches count on, or rather, live for. Creatures who are boys at the conclusion of one season are destined to become superhero adolescents by the beginning of the next.

Even Sam, who'd hovered always near the 50th percentile on his pediatrician's growth chart, measured in above five feet at the Indians' first practice of the 2001 season. Though he remained slender and smooth faced, he'd finally begun to regain his old baseball confidence. "Sam's been crushing the ball in practice," Coach Robert reported to me over the phone. This, he knew, would be a favorable entrée to our conversation, the point of which was to ask if I would be the team mom, a request I'd expected was forthcoming. What a cinch! I was neither pregnant nor nursing a baby that season. Plus, Robert knew all about our off-season construction project and was thus counting on me to host lots of supplementary BP sessions for the Indians.

Which I did, and the Indians responded well; the team seemed to gel during this second season and enjoyed many victories. As for Sam, by mid-April, his orange bar on Houston's computer graph had grown fat and long. As the season waned, it actually extended beyond those of even the perennial all-stars who were his teammates. And his purple bar (HRSP that is, or Hits with Runners in Scoring Position) was off the chart.

Thus did he and the Indians surge to a strong finish, while my second born, Matt, slugged happily away in the AA League. For her part, Emma was six and could entertain herself with other siblings and walk unassisted to the concession stand to place her order. Ian at two was a regular on the park's playscape yet still content to be left behind with his indulgent sitter if we had a crucial game that demanded my full attention. What bliss! I never *once* considered the option of conceiving another son but simply basked in the glory of all things Little League—the sunny Atlanta spring, the repeated ping of bat on happy ball, the smells of dewy grass and honeysuckle.

I should have known better.

Ten days before the playoffs, square in the middle of the Indians' longest winning streak of the season, I received a phone call from the nurse at Sam's school.

"Mrs. Payne?"

"Yes?"

"This is Mrs. Reynolds in the school infirmary."

Oh, Lord, I thought, *he's got a fever and will have to come home and there goes the rest of my day, and anyway, will he be able to play in his game tomorrow?*

"Now I don't want you to worry."

Worry? What—was he having an asthma attack? Or, convulsing?!

"Yes??"

"There's been an accident, and I've got Sam here with me."

"An *accident?*"

"Yes, and he's fine! But I do think he should see an orthopedist."

Well, that ought to be easy but ... no! Not an orthopedist! Not with the playoffs so close at hand!

"What happened?"

"Well, it's a little unclear ..."

Is it ever any other way with boys and accidents?

"But it seems he and some buddies were wrestling outside after lunch, and, well, one of them came down pretty hard on Sam's leg."

"And that buddy was?"

Pause.

"Um, it was Sean Lewis, Mrs. Payne."

"Oh," I whimpered, heart thudding. Sean Lewis was, of course, the largest boy in the sixth grade. He excelled on the football field where he played guard and where his teammates had nicknamed him "Terminator" on account of the way he could neutralize opposing players.

"I'll be right there."

Sam's injury became a great orthopedic mystery. His X-rays were clear, and the site of the blow didn't swell much, yet for a week or so, he walked with crutches, pampering his right leg like a crumpled wing. He missed a few games yet managed (with a certain amount of encouragement from his mother) to finish out the season and enter the playoffs wearing a leg brace specially fashioned by his father. By the second round of the playoffs, his limp had diminished to a hitch, but he continued to wear his brace in the effort to avoid re-injury.

It was a warm, sun-splashed day in May, and I had coerced my parents into coming out to watch the boys, who had overlapping games. My mother, who has little patience with sports, did like to do her grandparental duty by attending the odd extra-curricular event now and then. Never wanting to risk being accused of *favoritism*, she preferred to attend a game for Sam here, a school play for Matt there, a dance recital for cousin Casey there. With time and age, this grew a bit dicey. How could she, by then approaching her mid-eighties, possibly achieve equity with sixteen grandchildren and four great-grands living in six different states? This mind-boggling situation, in tandem with the Alzheimer's symptoms my father suffered during the last years before his death in 2003, all but froze her out of leaving the house for long stretches of time.

So I figured this two-for-one afternoon at Buckhead Baseball offered a handy way to check two kids off the guilt list for the price of one. My mother had complied, and my father, deeply entrenched by then in the mysterious workings of his own mind, went wherever he was told. Once upon a more lucid time, he and I had shared a love of baseball, and though he had never played the game, he had in his youth been a skilled athlete, quick with natural coordination and a slender, graceful build that had everything to do, genetically speaking, with Sam's success in sports. I liked to think, then, that watching his grandsons play might soothe my father's life-weariness, maybe help him focus his splintered consciousness.

As a rule, I disliked when the boys' games overlapped, much preferring to have them play consecutively (doesn't every parent?) so that I might watch the entirety of each one, but considering Sam's quick recovery from his injury, I hardly had room to complain. Too, the Majors and AA fields at Buckhead Baseball happen to lie adjacent to one another, with the right field corner of the AA field backing up to the Majors' left field corner. A walking path meanders between, providing the perfect spot for a devoted parent such as myself to unfold a lawn chair between the fences and enjoy a decent view of each game.

On that day, I lugged not one but *three* chairs out to this favorite spot, my parents making their arduous way behind me. Emma scuttled off to the playground, and by the time we set up our little family camp, both games were under way. The Indians faced one of the League's top teams, the Orioles, in the second round of a double elimination tournament, whereas Matt's team, the Bulls, had played their way into the AA semifinals.

Although the Bulls were overmatched, I took solace in Matt's achieving a couple of personal triumphs. For months he'd been slowly, sometimes reluctantly, settling in to the position of catcher. It was a hard and dirty job, but a lover of drama in all its forms, Matt enjoyed wearing the personality-altering face mask and donning the other cool gear required of the position. By this late-season game, he'd even begun to get the hang of actually *catching*. In the third inning, a batter tried to bunt for a hit, and he serenely threw the runner out at first. A few plays later, he caught a pop-up behind the plate, only to receive a standing ovation.

Squeezing my father's mottled wrist, I asked gently, "Did you *see* that, Pop?" It seemed certain he had; he was staring at home plate with a sweet, satisfied grin on his face.

"Hmmm?" he answered, tired eyes searching the field for some familiar landmark. "Who's that out *there*?" he asked, lifting a crooked finger towards the runner on first. "Is that Sam?"

"No, Pop," I screamed now at the side of his head. He was deaf as an old oak. "But that's Matt catching." I tugged on his arm, hoping to force a turn of his head. "He just caught a pop-up!"

"Izzat right?" he asked, this man who had graduated with the highest average in his class at Georgia Tech. Excited in spite of himself, he faced me and smiled, milky-brown eyes warm and grateful.

"He didn't see it," snapped my mother. "Now what was it Matt did?"

"Oh, sure!" Pop perked up, gazing proudly at the runner on first again. "*There's* Matt. What position did you say he plays?"

"He's over there!" my mother cried, giving him a little slug to direct his attention towards home plate.

"Catcher, Pop," I said, smiling and rubbing his knee. "Matt's the *catcher*."

My mother sighed.

"Gotten right tall, hasn't he?"

The runner on first, he meant.

By the fifth inning of the Bulls' game, the score in the Indians-Orioles game was tied 3-3 in the fourth. Matt was due up, and Sam, who'd grounded out with runners on in his previous plate appearance, would bat late in the inning *if* we managed to get anyone on base. Inning to inning, I'd been realigning my lawn chair and now faced the AA field again, knowing I couldn't miss what would probably be Matt's final chance to hit of the season, yet I jumped at any hint of action on the Majors' field. My parents' chairs remained in a sort of asymmetrical limbo. If Mom watched too closely, she grew upset anyway, worrying about all the boys who struck out or made errors. My father, as you might imagine, was content to bask, turtle-like, in the Atlanta sunshine he'd loved for four score and some odd years.

The Indians managed a base on balls, a couple hits between outs, and I grew dizzy, not only from turning back and forth while providing my parents a play-by-play that neither of them paid a spot of attention to, but because it came to pass that my sons would step up to bat at precisely the same moment. Each took his practice swings and settled into his respective stance, Matt's a deep muscular crouch designed to take advantage of his strength and size, and Sam's the relaxed upright posture of a lean left-hander. I watched him for a moment, the easy lankiness in his body offsetting the intensity of his concentration, and thought of how much he resembled his grandfather, whose focus may have begun to wane but whose long, lanky legs stretched out just then beside mine. Time was, he could swing the bat with similar grace, back when our family played beach whiffle ball during family vacations.

Then I panicked—*would I be able to see both my boys hit? Could I trust Mom to watch one of them and give a reliable report?* (I wasn't at all confident she knew the difference between a ball and a strike.) Should I climb the hill behind the fields in order to see them both at once? With this ludicrous thought, I stepped back and nearly toppled over Emma.

"Mommy! Sam's up!" she cried, out of breath.

"I know, sweetie. Matt, too! And I can't see both at the same time!"

"That's OK. I'll watch Sam for you."

That could work! I certainly felt more confident in my six-year-old daughter than in the other present options. Although I longed to observe each boy for myself (*what if they both hit home runs?*), this second set of eyes seemed my best hope.

"Good idea, honey," I said, chewing a nail. "Tell me when each pitch is coming." Which she did, like a regular Harry Caray.

The count on Matt inched up to two and two and ran full on Sam. About this time my mother turned to compliment Emma on the jaunty little skirt she was wearing and happened to glance at Sam at the plate.

"What on earth is that on Sam's leg?" she asked.

"Just a brace, Mom."

"A brace? Is he still *injured?*"

"It's OK. It's much better."

"Well, it must *not* be OK if he's in a brace. I do not believe in letting children play injured. You could be doing him permanent damage."

The pitcher hurled a fastball. Matt swung hard and crushed a hit just as Emma yanked my arm.

"Mommy! Mommy!" she cried. "Here it comes again!" and I turned in time to see Sam catch air for his third strike. *Drat*, I thought but felt suddenly unburdened. I took Emma's hand and ran, dragging her past my mother, still ranting about Sam's leg, and over to the AA fence. In pursuit of Matt's hit, the center fielder ran full tilt, neck craning to see the ball as it outdistanced him, bouncing only once in its journey to the outfield fence. Matt rounded second, a grin spreading across his face.

"That was good, right, Mommy?" Emma asked, clapping and wearing a generous smile herself.

"That was *very* good," I assured her.

"Yay, *Matt*! Yay!" my mother screamed, popping up beside us and clapping heatedly. "He's such a good hitter!" she exclaimed, as if *she* were Harry Caray himself.

I patted her on the back then went to retrieve my father who had evacuated his chair and was gathering bits of trash near the Majors' field. Always a neat freak, he'd lately become a regular sanitation worker, loving to escape my mother's watchful eye wherever we might be in order to collect the nastiest of cups and greasiest of fast-food bags. I gingerly grasped his hand just before he could nab an oozing rotten apple and settled him back in his seat, then fell into my own. To think, to breathe. One for two wasn't so bad, really. *And how like Little League!* How wrenching was the sight of Sam striking out at such a crucial juncture in his game, yet how my heart soared to see Matt hustling proudly into third base. Did it matter that in the long run *his* hit was of no consequence to his team? Did it matter that Sam's failure at the plate might lead to his team being eliminated from the playoffs? Did *any* of this matter enough to warrant such a swell of emotion?

Still at the fence, Emma and my mother gestured madly, shouting to get Matt's attention, something he clearly wasn't in the mood to give. Hands trembling, my father fingered the souvenir cup I'd handed him in place of the soiled one we'd tossed away. I rested my hand on his shoulder and surveyed this park I'd come to know so well. Ancient oak trees on the hillside behind us shifted in a pungent breeze. The sun, so warm on my neck and shoulders, blazed over the bleachers, swarming with parents and friends. Little boys in grimy, untucked jerseys took turns chucking a tennis ball against the back of the AA dugout in a frenzied game of their own invention. Near the concession stand, a huddle of girls, mostly Emma's buddies, played in a pile of spare infield dirt, pushing up hills and digging tunnels to serve as a palace for their Barbie dolls, while yet another group of boys, older, surrounded one of Buckhead's legendary coaches, Coach Bill, who'd been managing teams for fifteen years. Coach Bill had lost an eye in an accident a couple years earlier, and from the sound of the boys' raucous laughter, I figured he was popping in his *glass* eye, the one done up us a white ball with red stitching and a *B* in fancy cursive.

Slowly, a kind of joy seeped into my muddled brain. Rumbling along behind me, Coach Jim Loyd, the Majors Pirates' manager and long-time groundskeeper for the park, maneuvered his tractor between pockets of fans cheering or laughing or munching peanuts. Wearing the limp T-shirt and overalls that were his trademark on days when the Pirates' had no game, Coach Loyd, his tanned face bristly with whiskers and lined from so many seasons under the sun, nodded my way, tipped his cap at my mother and continued on his journey towards the Rookie field, empty for the moment and in need of sprucing up before its next game.

Maybe it all mattered, a little. This touch of early summer heat, this smell of freshly mown grass tinged with the scent of hot dogs, these squeals of children and this commotion of grandparents and the easy banter of friends young and old just being together, relaxed, for an hour or two. That park, that day, and all our days there.

◆   ◆   ◆

The Indians later took the lead, and in spite of his ailing leg, Sam hit a double to knock in the winning run. The Indians fought their way into the championship game, where they faced Jim Loyd and his Pirates. Sadly for the Indians, these Pirates, who had played their way out of the losers' bracket, had become a team of destiny—kind of like the 2004 Red Sox who finally broke the curse of the Babe by winning eight straight playoff games. Coach Loyd, who had been coaching Pirates' teams for seventeen long dusty years, had never come away with a trophy. His 2001 team had given him his best season to date, and everyone involved with Buckhead Baseball, save those of us related by blood to the Indians' players, was pulling for a Pirates' victory. Not only that (or maybe because of that), our bats, so thunderous in their power for so long, grew hauntingly silent against the Pirates' pitching.

We lost the championship in a rather undistinguished contest. After the game, our boys glumly accepted their runner-up trophies, then listened as Coach Loyd congratulated his winning players. As he spoke, his tough, leathery hands caressed the noble gold ballplayer atop the oversized trophy which he would be able to admire daily in the equipment room. So gruff and masculine, Coach Loyd cried as he hugged each of his boys. The Indians had come so far and losing was no fun, but even I had to admit it seemed OK to have lost to these long-suffering Pirates.

That evening, Coach Robert nominated Sam for the Twelve-Year-Old All-Star Tournament Team. Scheduled to attend a long session of camp, Sam nevertheless decided to go for it.

THE BOYS OF SUMMER

While the Indians' made their ill-fated run at the championship, summer crept upon us. The days grew long and lazy as the pulse of our family life ticked back a notch. I alone continued to fret over Little League. The children played in the sprinkler or lingered over board games; I worried Sam might be passed over in what everyone knew would be a tense all-star selection process. The children, exhausted by hours of sun and underwater play, plunged deep into sleep when their heads hit their pillows each night; I lay in bed weighing Sam's chances: Would the all-star coaches be anxious about his leg injury? Would they dare choose a player like Sam, who had limited all-star experience, over seasoned players who'd been all-stars for years?

On the night of the final vote, we ate dinner early, outside on the deck. It was a clear and balmy June night, and before they'd swallowed their last bites, Sam and Matt pleaded to be dismissed for a game of *Manhunt* on the cul-de-sac around the corner. I excused them, then nervous about the phone ringing (or not), busied myself with bathing Ian and putting him to bed. By 8:30, Houston was catching up on paperwork while Emma, her eyes heavy, watched her video of *Cinderella* for the thirty-third time. I sat at the kitchen table paying bills, the back door flung open to a soft breeze. Out back, a breath of sunlight hovered in the trees where a cluster of fireflies began their slow circular dance up through the branches.

Finally, the phone rang. Stomach churning, I punched the TALK button.

"Is Sam home?"

"No!" I fairly shouted.

Taken aback, Coach Gip identified himself and asked, "You think he's up for a summer of baseball?"

A summer of baseball, the phrase settled like a balm over my restless spirit. But was this, you might wonder, the same Coach Gip? (Could there possibly be *two*?) One and the same—this was Coach Gip of the Yankees, the very one who'd humiliated Sam on the mound when he was eleven. Just goes to show you. Though my full forgiveness for his assault on my son's ego was long in coming, by the conclusion of Sam's twelve-year-old season, even I had to admit that Gip had become Sam's strongest ally.

As he does each year, during the last third of the season, Gip attended many Majors' games other than his own. Sure, he was scouting for his all-star team, but he took care as he watched to congratulate weaker players when they improved and to compliment their parents. Gip had been there to see Sam play through his injury, took note as he hustled up the base paths, hobbling on his gimpy leg. He knew Sam had led the Indians deep into the playoffs, not with power, but with smart, creative hitting, solid fielding, and a drive to win.

But because of his small stature and his shaky tournament team history, Sam at twelve remained a long shot as an all-star. Two other Indians had also been nominated, boys who were perennial all-stars. Because there are ten Majors' teams to choose from, it's rare for more than two boys per team to make the cut of twelve players. Yet Gip believed. I learned later that during the discussion session that preceded the final all-star vote, Coach Gip had faced great resistance to the idea of taking Sam on the team and thus displacing one of the repeat players. Yet, since he was to be the manager of the tournament team, the one to mold and develop these boys into a bunch of competitors, Gip's vote carried great weight. In the end, he railroaded Sam in.

At the time of Gip's call, I understood little of this, but I'd already begun to sense that no matter what he thought of his pitching limitations, this man was on Sam's side. And that seemed enough.

"He made it!" I shouted, slamming down the phone. Hurrying towards Houston's study, I was blindsided by Matt, bounding through the front door, breathless, with Sam fast behind.

"Sorry, Mom! We lost track of time!"

Was it past their curfew? I hadn't noticed, but I stiffened, resisting an urge to hug them both, so captivating was their energy, so endearing their ruddy cheeks, damp and clammy from their hustle home. I breathed in the sweet smell of boy after a raucous night of summer play then quizzed Sam.

"Didn't you take a watch?"

He mumbled a half-baked excuse.

"Well, pay closer attention next time," I said, pausing for a moment to savor the look of woeful innocence on their boyish faces. They squirmed. *Was I going to dismiss them? Punish them?*

Houston wandered into the hall. I seized the moment.

"Guess what, Sam?"

He looked to his father for a clue.

"What?" he asked, frowning, expecting the worst.

"You made all-stars."

"I did?" he asked, smothering a smile, trying to remain nonchalant as a good almost-thirteen-year-old should. "Did somebody call?"

"Coach Gip," I said.

"Way to go, bud!" said Houston, wrapping Sam in a bear hug.

"Cool," Sam replied, wiggling away in order to return Matt's high five. He then ran through the house, leaping high under each doorjamb in the effort to touch the top and prove he'd grown since his last trip through.

First thing the next morning, I called the director of the boys' camp to inform him Sam would be arriving sometime after their official start date of July 3.

"He's playing on a baseball tournament team," I chirped, perhaps a bit heavy on the enthusiasm.

"How wonderful for him," he said. "And when *can* we expect him?"

"Well, it could be as soon as the ninth or tenth!" I ventured, knowing full well that it could just as easily be as late as the fifteenth, or that Sam might miss camp altogether. The district tournament didn't even start until July seventh, and if the team played well, they could advance to the state tournament, then the region … and, of course, with a little luck, they might play their way into the Little League World Series in Williamsport, Pennsylvania (which didn't get underway until mid-August). OK, that would require a Babe Ruth-sized portion of luck, but you never know! Still, planning for such a glorious tournament season could only jinx the team's chances—better to announce Sam's camp arrival based on our not winning a single game.

"OK, Mrs. Payne, just let us know as soon as you can."

"Of course! We'll get him there pronto when he's done playing!"

With that, I hung up. Sweating now with self-doubt, I examined my motives. Here I was postponing Sam's going to camp—a camp that didn't seem to have a session *long* enough for his taste—where he would no doubt be poised to absorb countless lessons in self-reliance and problem solving in the cool, unsullied air of the Appalachian mountains. Instead, Sam would enjoy a month of daily four-hour baseball practices in Atlanta's sweltering, smoggy heat, practices that *could* result (perish the thought) in the tournament team playing only a handful of games together. Throw in the fact that we were forfeiting around $75 for each day of camp missed and, well, *whatever would Dr. Spock say?*

Then again, a kid only gets one chance to go the Little League World Series—many a boy would have traded a lifetime supply of s'mores for Sam's spot.

"Who was on the phone, Mom?" Matt asked, wandering into the kitchen. Sam's becoming an all-star would mean he would have to go to camp on his own for the first time. He was a child somewhat prone to homesickness, and the previous year, it had helped that Sam was just a few cabins away. Needless to say, I had yet to share with him the news of Sam's delayed arrival.

"Oh, that was the director at High Rocks."

"Are we still going to camp?" he asked, a trace of worry *(or was it hope?)* in his voice.

"Sure you are! I just had to let them know Sam might be a few days late getting there."

"He will? For baseball? So am I going late, too?"

"No, honey. The camp thinks it's best for you to start with all the others, since you're younger. But Sam won't be long getting there!"

"Oh. Okay," Matt said, his tender hazel eyes focused on his feet and his baby-fat cheeks coloring.

"I'm going outside," he added brushing by me, eyes hidden behind his straight dark bangs. My impulse again was to reach out and embrace him, but he gave me that I'm-too-big-for-such-nonsense shrug as he went. Instead, to my growing list of parental concerns, I added a hefty dose of worry that Matt wasn't really the camp type at all.

◆   ◆   ◆

The All-Star Bucks practiced long and hard, often simulating infield situations and running the bases until well past dark. Most mornings I let Sam sleep in while I dropped Emma and Ian off at their respective day camps. Even so, because Sam couldn't be allowed to swim, or sweat, or expend a drop of potential baseball energy before practice time, he and I were often stuck as housemates.

"Want me to crack the eggs, Mom?" he surprised me by asking on our second morning alone together. I'd just walked in the door and didn't have nearly enough caffeine in my system to have mapped out a breakfast plan. *Did I even have eggs?* We'd had them scrambled with cheese the day before, but Sam looked so enthusiastic over the idea of a repeat eggy feast, I crossed my fingers and chimed in.

"Sure! How 'bout an omelet?"

With this, he turned from the fridge where he'd been scanning for eggs.

"Do you know *how?*" he asked, and Sam, the same Sam who for over a year had rarely gazed upon me with anything but embarrassment for my shortcomings or total exasperation with my overall life philosophy, looked at me with awe. Domestic slacker that I was, I suppose the only omelets I'd ever provided my kids were those prepared at the Waffle House.

"I do!" I said, leaning around him to check the eggs—three left, *bingo!*

"Pull out the butter and cheese. And bacon maybe?"

"Yeah, Mom. Duh."

Thus did we fall into a happy routine. During the next few days, we made it all: grits, hash browns, sausage, biscuits—I became a short-order specialist, and all the while Sam and I were beating and stirring and frying, we talked. We talked baseball mainly—about how he'd managed to land the starting spot in center field after starting as a sub in left, about his disappointment at being given the last spot in the batting order (again), about the Braves and whether they'd get the chance to put the Yankees in their place come October. When a weepy letter arrived from Matt at camp, Sam even offered his perspective on homesickness.

We had only about a week of this, yet it sufficed. Perhaps Sam will one day remember that when he was smaller with a gentler fastball, I was actually able to catch when he wanted to practice pitching. Perhaps he'll recall those spring afternoons in

Augusta, Georgia, when I tossed endless whiffle balls for him to launch into the sky. Perhaps he won't. But of one thing I'm sure. During that summer he was twelve, he realized that his nosy, annoying, fanatical mother could talk sports. And through all the perilous, unpredictable, heartbreaking teen years that loomed ahead, we could always find each other at the far side of a box score.

◆   ◆   ◆

Georgia's District Nine Twelve Year Old All-Star Tournament traditionally begins on the first Saturday after the July Fourth holiday. Surely nothing more than coincidence determined that our 2001 Buckhead team drew a bye for the first round of games, but thanks to that bye, the Bucks opened their tournament season on Sunday, July 8, my forty-first birthday. We rose early that morning—we always rose early in those days before teenagers occupied most of the beds in our house. Ian was up by 6:30, and Emma came bounding in soon after, chanting the birthday song, ignorant of the fact that Daddy had just slipped out of the room with the baby to give mom another thirty minutes of sleep.

I suppose turning forty-one is special, in an offhand way, the way perhaps that Flag Day is special. You might notice the existence of such a day and feel a flash of affection for it when you flip the page on your organizer, but does anyone get really energized about such a birthday? Propped up on one elbow, I smiled during Emma's shrill rendition then gave her a kiss. But after Houston fetched her away, I fell back on the pillow feeling grim. At least when I'd turned forty, somebody had invited me out for sympathy lunch and staked a sign in our yard that read, "Lordy, Lordy, Martha's Forty." All forty-one seemed good for was confirming the raw truth of middle age.

But this was a baseball day! With that in mind, I could face anything—Myopia? Cellulite? Saddle bags under the eyes? No worries. Middle-aged or not, I would soon be watching Sam fulfill his (*my?*) dream—playing with the twelve-year-old all-stars, the elite of Little League. The Weather Channel forecast for the eighth read simply HOT in bright orange, complete with those little wavy lines radiating from the letters. Low nineties, in fact, were broadcast for Sam's game time, which accounted for Emma's request that she be allowed to play at a friend's rather than cheer on her brother. Ian, too, we decided, would be better off napping at home, so Mom might enjoy a game in peace on her special day.

Sam and I set out for Murphey-Candler Park, ironically the same Little League park where he'd played rather unremarkably in his only other district tournament appearance. Reversing the sociability of our recent breakfasts, Sam spoke hardly at all during our twenty-minute drive around I-285. Always superstitious about sports, maybe he was remembering his poor performance as a nine-year-old and worrying over a jinx. Or maybe he was feeling just a tad *inept*. Word was that during the Bucks' final batting practice, every last player *except* Sam had hit a home run.

Sam had broken this news to me as I tucked him in bed the night before.

"You know what they say!" I gushed. "Bad practice makes for a good show!"

"Yeah. Right, Mom," Sam said, his green eyes leering. "Good *night.*"

And with that, he'd tugged knees to belly and pulled the covers over his head. *Feeling inept* perhaps fails to impart the level of his anxiety. Relentless, his Little League roller coaster raced on. Despite his late-season heroics and Coach Gip's faith in his bat, he'd been judged one of the weaker hitters on a team most considered mediocre in the first place. Few Buckhead fans expected our boys to win the district tournament. In fact, their coaches, having been given what they saw as an average bunch of players, had employed a psych-up strategy that many an all-star parent would question over the next few days.

"You guys *suck*," had asserted Coach Duke, one of the tournament team's veteran assistant coaches, on but the second day of practice. "You know that's what everybody says about you."

Such esteem building! Now why was it Sam was skipping camp?

"Let's get out there and kick some butt and show them what we're really made of!"

A certain reverse psychology, I suppose, and though many of the mothers bristled to hear it, *We suck!* became sort of a rallying cry for the Bucks, a turn of phrase they chanted often on the way to practice—you know, to fire each other up. The whole strategy seemed to work for Sam, who for whatever reason wasn't bothered by a little cussing and yelling.

"It just makes me mad, Mom. We *have* to prove them wrong."

A model player attitude for Coach Duke—no doubt he would use Sam as a teaching tool in future coaching clinics.

So after weeks of toiling in order to show the Little League world their true grit, the Buckhead All-Stars finally arrived at their big day. Whereas most of their buddies had hung up their caps for good when the regular season ended, these boys had been given the honor of playing into the summer, of playing for as long as they could win, of going all the way to the Little League World Series and *playing before the world on television* ... if only they could win a few baseball games. Sure, they weren't the most talented group ever to represent Buckhead, but they'd all been playing baseball for seven years now. They'd won plenty of games; all they needed was to win seven or eight more.

As I lurched to a stop beside the Murphey-Candler fields, I glanced at Sam. With the fingers of his left hand, bronzed from his endless practice season, he drummed his knee, which jiggled up and down, up and down. Once pudgy at the knuckles, these fingers had shed their childish curves and seemed impossibly long. As he lunged to step out of his seat, his all-star pinstripes stretching just so over his thin, coltish legs, I marveled at his hair, recently grown long and wild, too bushy to be contained by his cap, that almighty cap inscribed with a *B* for Buckhead.

"Hit 'em hard, buddy," I suggested and received a mere, "OK," as he gathered his bat bag from the way back. In the rear-view mirror, I watched his mouth clench with the effort of hoisting bag to shoulder. When he looked up, it was with nervous, troubled eyes. He might as well have worn a sign: *I'm the ninth batter—no one expects me to hit hard!*

"Good luck," I added.

"Thanks, Mom." The door slammed, and he strode off.

The air was so thick and still and the opposing pitcher so large and menacing during warm-ups that I decided against watching all of Sam's pregame activities and motored down to a nearby Starbuck's for a therapeutic coffee. I returned a few minutes before game time to find the Bucks safe in their dugout, chomping gum and laughing.

But where was Sam?

Ah, *there*, at the far end of the dugout, framed by a square of chain-link fencing where the on-deck batters would take their practice swings. He stood with his back to me, the number *3* emblazoned across his red jersey below PAYNE in blue block letters. Facing him, standing close as a lover, his forearms draped over Sam's shoulders, was Coach Gip. Hands on his hips, Sam gazed up into Gip's eyes, just inches away from his own.

What was he saying to my son, this man who'd once allowed his Yankees to rip hit after hit off of Sam on the mound, stealing a humiliating number of bases and generally demoralizing him? In his stance, in the intensity of his gaze, I could see how much Gip now cared—not just about winning but about Sam as a human being. Maybe what he told Sam that day was altogether ordinary, possibly little more than a reminder about signs. But something about his posture, the way he leaned in so close, suggested an intimacy, that peculiar male intimacy that flourishes only on the athletic field, where men and boys alike communicate in a way that mothers can't help but envy. *What* Gip said didn't matter. It was the spirit of his words, more importantly his touch, that I'm sure played a part in the way the game unfolded that day. I snapped a photo of this scene, one saved for posterity in Sam's album of life-altering moments.

Feeling queasy after gulping down my frappucino, I donned my Buckhead cap, greeted my fellow parents, then scanned for a couple of bleacher seats slightly apart from the crowd. Houston called to say he was running late, so I settled in a spot and tossed my purse into the next seat over. A hot gust of wind blew up a twister of infield dirt that swept across the bleachers, raising a collective yelp from the moms. Was it my imagination, or weren't the fields at Murphey-Candler always drier, dustier, harder even, than ours at Buckhead?

I chafed in my bleacher seat, sweat dripping down my neck, and watched our boys jog out to the third-base line as the tournament's master of ceremonies announced each name and position. Sure it was rinky-dink, but I still felt a thrill as Sam hustled out to the sounds of, "Number 3, the center fielder, Sam Payne!" Once their coaches had joined them, the boys could hardly stand still. Uneasy, bothered by heat and nerves, they fidgeted, socking each other in the arm and chuckling while the Murphey-Candler Mavericks took their bows. After fudging his way through the *Star Spangled Banner* and the Little League Pledge, Sam bolted for the dugout.

The Bucks went three up, three down, in the top of the first. Squirming and wiping our brows, we parents chalked this up to all-star jitters and watched expectantly as the boys huddled together outside their dugout, gloves in hand. "Goooooo Buckhead!" they chanted, just after reminding each other, I'm sure, of how much they sucked, then broke for the field. There, out in front, was my brave boy, trotting out to center field. On the mound for Buckhead was a boy who appeared to be two years older than Sam. Yes, even our sorry little team could boast of one player whose birth certificate opposing parents might demand to see. At age twelve, the fuzzy-lipped Mike Cramer measured in at five feet seven inches. He threw hard although he had some, *well*, focus problems and couldn't always be counted on to react predictably, when a batter bunted, for example. And then there were some control issues....

But Mike looked good as he took his final warm-up pitches. All the Bucks looked good, relaxed even. Sam and his outfield cronies clowned around, diving and rolling on the grass while they shagged flies. The infielders threw with grace, hitting all their intended targets. We were making a statement, warming up with authority. *We'll just see who sucks in the end!*

When Mike's first pitch to Murphey-Candler's leadoff batter burned a path through the strike zone, our bleachers rumbled with applause. I allowed myself to hope, to dream of making it to the state tournament ... but on the next pitch, the batter connected and hit a short fly ball to, where else? Center field. Sam (who never has focus problems) glanced skyward in shock, broke back a few steps, then had to hustle in and play the hit off the bounce. Not only that, he overthrew his cutoff man, insuring that the runner made it to second.

I sank deep into my seat, trying to avoid the melancholy nod of one particular mother a few seats away, the one who never missed a chance to gaze forlornly at the parent of an erring player. The official scorer gave the boy a double, but everyone knew Sam would have caught the ball if not for his mental mistake. As nearly always happens, this leadoff hitter ended up scoring on a steal and a hit by the number three batter. When the inning closed, Buckhead trailed 1-0.

The top of the second brought an instant replay of the first with the Bucks pasting a few more zeros onto their line score—no runs, no hits, no base runners even. Six up, six down, for our offense. *Was this a self-fulfilling prophecy?* Still feeling squeamish about Sam's costly error, I wandered over to sit with Annie, Walter's mom—Annie, whom I had dubbed (with only a touch of envy) Mrs. Been There, Done That, back when I was but a fledgling all-star mom. Walter, the Bucks' shortstop, had just struck out, and I figured her misery might like some company. She looked up at me with the sagging, cloudy eyes that are the trademark of every mother whose son has ever struck out in a big game, which, of course, means, every Little League mother.

"Tough pitcher," I offered, but she would have none of that.

"Oh, heck," Annie spat, her voice tinny with frustration. "Maybe Gip should have them all bunt."

"At least Walter's been solid in the field."

"Oh, Sam did fine on that play!" she gushed, but her forced enthusiasm made me feel all the worse.

Houston wandered up just then, a smile on his face.

"Wow! Good game, huh?" he asked, coercing me to realize that it was, after all, only 1-0, and we had four at-bats remaining. *Anything could happen!* If only that one run hadn't resulted from a misstep by our son.

I reviewed for him the play-by-play, but he refused to join in my despair.

"We haven't even batted through the order yet," he reminded me, by which he meant Sam hadn't batted yet.

Still, I found myself suffering from the same worries I'd tried to purge Sam of earlier. Would he, the number nine batter, be able to hit this pitcher if his more powerful teammates couldn't? *He might.* My left brain *knew* that the one sure thing about Little League was its unpredictability, its potential for making heroes out of the little guys. But who could think rationally when the sun was so blasted hot, the humidity so syrupy, the image of Sam's blunder etched so deeply in my *right* brain?

In the bottom of the second, Murphey-Candler's number-five hitter sent a ball halfway into the next county, and Buckhead trailed 2-0. *No problem!* Our seven, eight, and nine hitters were due up! And lo and behold, they came through. Seven and eight reached base safely and after ticking up two strikes, Sam fouled off four pitches then finally hit a hard grounder back up the middle—one of his signature hits, not the work of a power hitter, but it did the trick. He'd redeemed himself, atoned for the run he'd allowed to score earlier. The top of our order kept the rally going, and by the middle of the third, Buckhead led 4-2 with the fourth run scoring thanks to a hit by Annie's son, Walter.

She and I hugged and cried then fell exhausted into our seats.

"That did NOT suck," I whispered, and we laughed, loose and giddy as a couple of high school cheerleaders.

"I told you two not to worry," Houston said, just before he left to join a couple of dads along the third-base line, feeling, no doubt, that he'd supported me in my time of trouble and could then safely escape the torrent of my emotions.

It was a good thing he left. Although Mike and the Bucks held the Mavericks scoreless in the third and fourth, our boys couldn't score a single insurance run, and I began to fret. Sure, we were winning by two, but as the home team, Murphey-Candler had the advantage of the final at-bat. Plus, they were merely up against the wretched 2001 Boys from Buckhead. *We needed a ten-run lead!*

As the game stretched into the bottom of the fifth, I couldn't shake a feeling of doom in the pit of my stomach. Rather than burden Annie with my negative energy, I began to wander the field. From the right-field corner, I watched the Mavericks' leadoff man knock a single. From the third-base line, I saw their next batter draw a walk. I then circled back around home plate to my seat, avoiding the center field fence lest my bad karma should rub off on Sam and force another error.

Maybe I should have taken my karma to another galaxy. Sam, in fact, did not commit an error, perhaps only because the ball never came near him, but half of his teammates did. Mike should have been out of the inning, but we began hurling the ball willy-nilly, like it was a blistering lump of coal. It was the *Bad News Bears Take Atlanta*, and by the time the hysteria had simmered down, the score was tied, 4-4.

So much for birthday luck.

In the top of the sixth, Coach Gip adjusted his game plan. Sensing the inertia that had swept through his team, he played small ball. Our leadoff man bunted for a hit, advanced on a wild pitch, and made it to third on a bunt by our next batter, who reached first safely himself. With men on first and third and nobody out, that giant of a boy Mike Cramer stepped up to the plate.

"Base hit, Mikey!" called out Coach Bill, that one-eyed veteran coach who'd been helping the all-stars with their hitting. "Right here. Right *now*!"

Coach Bill sat just below me in the bleachers, directly behind home plate. A childless bachelor and a volunteer coach for over fifteen years in the AAA league, Coach Bill embodied the spirit of Little League. Though he stood to gain nothing, no one loved and encouraged his boys more than Coach Bill. He was never on the official roster of coaches for any all-star team, yet he helped teach hitting for almost all of them and never missed a tournament game at any level.

"Base hit, Mike. You can do this," Coach Bill reiterated, and Mike, really not a power hitter despite his size, seemed to loom large as a grizzly bear after hearing his voice. In came the pitch, and back up the middle went Mike's single, past the pitcher, and on into center field. One man scored and the Bucks had the lead again by one.

Mike beamed on first base, clapping unreservedly for himself, as the Buckhead parents cheered him on.

Next up, Eddie, our right fielder.

"Drive the ball, Eddie. Drive it!" chanted Coach Bill. "You're the man, Eddie!"

I could do no more than imitate and begged Eddie to drive one, too, between bouts of nail shredding, that is, since you-know-who was on deck. A nightmarish scene had already run through the movie projector in my mind—if an ill-wind should blow and Eddie should somehow hit into a double play, Sam would come up with two outs and a man on. Talk about pressure. *Drive it, Eddie.*

Eddie hit a grounder, *very* hard but within reach of the nimble Maverick shortstop. Thank God this boy did what every good Little Leaguer is programmed to do. He threw the ball to third, going for the sure out on the lead runner, rather than try for a double play. Sam then stepped up to bat facing the identical situation Eddie had—Bucks on first and second, his team up by one run but needing more, except for one thing—a wee little out now loomed on the scoreboard tally. A fresh mental horror show spun through my mind: *Sam* hits into a double play, thus ending the Bucks' chances for a big inning.

My nailbeds ached. I clasped my hands behind my back and tried to direct some positive vibes towards Sam at the plate. He stood in with confidence—not arrogance, mind you (compared to the oversized pitcher on the mound, Sam's ninety-five pound frame looked anything but menacing)—yet he stood tall in his

Buckhead jersey and wound his bat behind his head with just the right amount of tension in his shoulders. His right foot twitched slightly in anticipation of each pitch; his hands coiled loosely around his bat, same way they did when he and Matt launched tennis balls during games of home run derby in our backyard.

"Come on, Lassie!" called Coach Bill, remembering Sam's nickname. "You're a fighter!"

A rush of pride swept through me. *A fighter*, Coach Bill called him. *An overachiever, the Little Engine That Could.* But *could* he, in this impossibly stressful situation? I leaned against Annie, who held a tourniquet-like grip on my upper arm.

"He can do it," she assured me. Then louder, "*You* can do it, Sam!"

My head throbbed. I longed to cover my eyes. *Could somebody please tell me when it's over?* Instead I looked around for Houston. There he was, still down the third-base line. He caught my eye and raised a pair of crossed fingers.

First pitch, a ball. The concrete below my feet absorbed half the tension in my body. The significance of a first-pitch out of the strike zone cannot be underestimated. It leaves the pitcher off-guard, relaxes the batter just a hair. When the second pitch sailed wide of the plate, I felt light enough to levitate, if not for Annie, who with each pitch pressed the nails of her left hand more deeply into my inner elbow.

"Two and O!" she cried.

He might walk! And pass on responsibility for the game's outcome!

"Attaboy, Lassie! Way to watch!" called Coach Bill, turning to wink at me.

Next pitch, Sam watched when he shouldn't have. The umpire gave a guttural "Strike!" and I sponged all that excess tension right back up through my legs.

"Now you've seen one, Sam. *Drive* this one!" chanted Coach Bill. Lily-livered, I hid my face behind Annie's shoulder and rolled a few pills as the pitcher released the ball.

"Ping!" went the sound of bat on ball. I jerked my eyes back to the action.

Foul ball. Count—two and two.

Calgon—take me away! Those two opening balls had lost their value!

But here came another ball, high and outside. Sam lunged but held up. Full count, three balls, two strikes.

The nub of a nail back safely between my teeth, I began jumping repeatedly on the balls of my feet. "You can do it, Sam!" I squeaked.

"See the ball!" called Coach Bill. "You are a fighter!"

And fight Sam did, lacing one foul ball outside the third base line, then another just over the fence beyond the third-base bleachers. Sam was having what's known as a *good at-bat*—making contact, forcing a lot of pitches. I closed my eyes and breathed a prayer of thanks for this, then went ahead with a bribe. *Please God, if he could just avoid the double play.*

"Come on, Billy!" screamed the Mavericks' coach, shouting at his pitcher. "Number nine batter!" he continued. "He's *not* gonna hit it—just throw strikes!"

I flashed to a game—no a nightmare—that had come to pass over a year before when Gip in an earlier incarnation had spouted pitching insults with Sam on the mound. My cheeks flamed, my head reeled with anxiety and rage and wounded pride. How could this man, a stranger, say such a thing about my son?

"See the ball, Sam!" reaffirmed Coach Bill.

Hardened now, I couldn't even pray. The final pitch came fast, through the strike zone, but a touch low and inside. Sam swung. The ball flew off his bat towards right field. I clenched Annie's waist and traced its path, willing it to sail out of reach of the Mavericks' speedy right fielder, racing confidently towards the fence.

"Att-A-*Boy!*" howled Coach Bill, and I reeled, disbelieving what his confident tone implied. *Could it be?* The ball flew higher, buoyed up by the swell of cheers rising from our bleachers, then angled down towards the right field corner. A couple yards from the fence, the right fielder stutter-stepped, then stopped, as the ball disappeared beyond him.

Was that it? That flash of white skipping over the sidewalk just outside the fence?

I looked to the first-base umpire. His right hand held high, he extended his index finger, pointed toward the hazy blue sky, and spun his hand counterclockwise, mimicking the journey that even then, Sam was taking around the bases.

Cool as ever, Sam jogged around first, then second, but as he floated towards third, those vulnerable shoulders held tall and strong, his eyes and cheeks, even his chin, lifted into a broad smile. Coach Gip, grinning like the *Say-Hey* Kid, stepped out of the third-base coach's box for a high five, then gave Sam an extra slap on the rear as he coasted by.

Sam's teammates tumbled out of the dugout and up to the plate, where they crowded in, pumping their fists and shouting, "Laaa-sie! Laaa-sie!," all eyes on their number-nine batter as he trotted home.

MOPPING UP

All said, I enjoyed quite a send-off as I embarked on my forty-second trip around the sun. It would be poignant to think Sam had my birthday in mind when he knocked that ball out of the park, to imagine that when he stepped up to the plate with two men on, the notion may have whisked through his mind that he would get a big hit for Mom on her big day. I know better. Like any good ballplayer, he was thinking only of getting on base, of driving in a run or two for the good of his team.

"I'm *glad* the bases weren't loaded," he told Houston, who diverted him as he ambled off the field with Walter and a few others. "Then I would have been *trying* to hit a home run."

"No way, man. That never works!" Walter garbled through a wad of bubble gum.

"I know! You can't think about it!" said Sam, as if he'd been hitting home runs left and right for years.

By the time I raced down the bleachers to join the mob of well-wishers, he'd grown ill at ease. Blushing beneath his cap, he dropped his bat bag and mumbled thank-yous, sheepishly exchanging handshakes with Coach Bill and various team parents, parents who'd been watching him play baseball for nearly as long as I had. Breathless, I peered over Annie's shoulder, caught Sam's eye just as he leaned down to heave bat bag to shoulder once again.

The throng parted, and for a moment I felt somehow significant, validated, sort of like the Queen Mum. Jittery, tears imminent, I figured I'd better hug him quick. But as I lunged his way, arms outstretched, Sam stiffened and retreated, falling in beside Walter, his bat bag draped across his hip like a shield. My arms fell, mimicking my heart.

I got only a *Hey, Mom*, but he made eye contact and grinned large, and that would have to do. I smiled back, a tear or two bubbling up in spite of my determination to suppress them.

"Way to hit the ball," I said, stepping out of the congratulatory circle.

"Put that bag down and hug your mother," Houston commanded, his voice rising from behind, tinged with uncharacteristic gruffness. Sam shot him a pained look but complied, leaning into my loose embrace, bag swaying at his elbow.

"Aaaww," cooed Annie, who along with a few other parents had paused to observe this moment of maternal bliss. Much to Sam's relief, many of the Bucks themselves had long before bolted for the concession stand.

Sam's homer, which stretched the score comfortably to 8-4, had given Buckhead the insurance it needed to win that first game. In the bottom of the sixth, Coach Gip brought in a relief pitcher who was so fresh and pumped up he polished off the Mavericks, three up, three down. The memory of our boys' jubilant faces after this victory made tolerable the despair that would soon overtake us all. In game two, we lost irrevocably, managing only two hits against a daunting pitcher (with a full beard) and his team from Sandy Springs Little League, a team that would *in fact* go on to win the district, the state, *and* the Southern regional tournaments. Buckhead fell into the losers' bracket where we were forced to face again the Murphey-Candler Mavericks, only this time, a lust for revenge infused their bats while ours went cold.

So in the end, the Bucks sucked, and Sam made it to summer camp just over a week late, which provided Matt a dose of comfort and gave Sam's counselors plenty of time to shore him up with all those lessons in self-reliance he'd been missing out on.

On a muggy night in early August a few days after the boys returned home, our family gathered around the television to watch our foes from Sandy Springs play on ESPN2. We were gratified somehow to watch the pitcher who'd embarrassed our Bucks fan batter after batter from a team that must not have sucked at all, considering they'd earned the right to play on the screen before us. Although the boys from Sandy Springs didn't quite win the World Series, seeing their agile bodies, bodies we *knew* belonged to real flesh-and-blood boys, sprint and dive and laugh and cry on our television screen, soothed our battered egos.

Watching the Little League World Series has now become a family tradition. Many a hot August day I'll walk in the house, heart heavy with adult-sized worries and arms burdened with groceries, and demand help from the lanky, sweaty bodies sprawled across the furniture in our family room, only to receive, a "Mo-o-om, it's the Midwest playing New Mexico," or "Japan and Curacao are tied in the sixth!" Sometimes, this will be a replay of a game we've already seen, and everyone knows the outcome, but more often than not, I'll drop my bags, disregarding the softening ice cream, and perch on the arm of the couch, carefully avoiding the pair of sour athletic socks that happen to be attached to one of my teenagers' feet, in order to watch a group of lucky twelve-year-olds swing for the fences.

Matt, too, has completed his Little League career. He played in the Majors for Coach Loyd's Pirates. Underdogs during the regular season as Sam's Indians had been, his Pirates enjoyed a thrilling tournament season much like Sam's, and Matt had his share of heroic moments. He may try to play high school ball, he may not. Playing the electric guitar has become his passion. As for Sam at eighteen, though he's still lean and enjoys only average height, he loves the rough, exhilarating game of football. He spends a lot of time in the weight room, and come spring, he'll start in center field, maybe pitch a little in relief and swing his way through one final season of high school baseball.

I still go to his games. I go, that is, if I'm not needed to drive a soccer carpool for Ian or to take Matt to the orthodontist or Emma to a gymnastics meet. These games are fun. I wear with great pride my Wildcat Mom's button, the one that sports the number 3 (dubbed lucky ever since that home run) in Sam's school colors. But it's not the same. Emma and Ian come along most of the time—they love to play unsupervised in the school's high jump pit—but my mother never seems up to it now that my father is gone. So I sit rather still and prim on my bleacher cushion, clapping politely in an effort to keep my enthusiasm under wraps. There's somehow more tension among us parents, perhaps more at stake in these games played between boys who are nearly men. Or maybe it's less.

Or maybe I've learned a little something during my twelve years as a Little League mom—that winning is good but so is being there to see the boy who has yet to make contact with the ball finally get a hit; that having your child elected as an all-star is an honor and a delight until you get your heart broken from watching him fail; that even that heartbreak is something you don't want to miss, but that just as gratifying is the serenity that comes from sitting on the bleachers on a crisp, bright spring day, watching a bunch of future sluggers squeal and tumble across the tee-ball field before practice even starts.

I suppose there may be hope for me yet.

Just after Christmas each year, Ian, now seven, begins sleeping in old jerseys, sometimes his from tee-ball, sometimes one cast off years before by Sam or Matt. By mid-January, he begins counting the days until Opening Day, and now and then, he asks me for a game of catch. Last spring, he volunteered himself as the bat boy and number one cheerleader for Matt's Pony League team, and he can just about score a Braves' game all on his own. Matt claims he'd like to coach him one day, maybe once he progresses farther up Little League's competitive ladder, maybe in Kid Pitch, AA—where there's more at stake.

On the odd occasion when all the children are around the house on a clear day, the four of them sometimes organize a game of whiffle ball in the backyard. Sam and Matt, of course, are required to bat from the wrong side of the plate, and Emma often has to be restrained from turning cartwheels in the base paths. Other times, one of the big boys might throw with Ian or venture into the cage to pitch him tennis balls, many of which he hits deep into the net. But he whiffs his share, too, something that doesn't sit well with Sam, in particular.

"I don't know, Mom," he soberly reported, his voice deep and guttural, on a recent Sunday afternoon. "His hand-eye's good, but he's gotta learn to keep his weight back."

And I understood exactly what he meant.

Author's Note: After graduating from high school, Sam enrolled at Davidson College outside of Charlotte, North Carolina, and signed on to play outfield for the Division I Davidson Wildcats, making him an exception to the rule that only one out of every one hundred high school athletes goes on to play a collegiate sport.

For a few more seasons then, his mother, who is very proud, plans to be in the stands, cheering, every chance she gets.

978-0-595-42782-6
0-595-42782-0

CPSIA information can be obtained at www.ICGtesting.com
Printed in the USA
LVOW06s1336061015

457144LV00001BA/51/P